THE MONEY MURDERS

by Edgar-Award-winning author
FRANKLIN BANDY
as Eugene Franklin

𝔰𝔡

STEIN AND DAY/*Publishers*/**New York**

FIRST STEIN AND DAY PAPERBACK EDITION 1985
The Money Murders was originally published
by Stein and Day/*Publishers*.

Copyright © 1972 by Eugene Franklin
All rights reserved, Stein and Day, Incorporated
Designed by Louis A. Ditizio
Manufactured in the United States of America
Stein and Day/*Publishers*
Scarborough House
Briarcliff Manor, N.Y. 10510
ISBN 0-8128-8180-X

1

For a woman who had just embezzled ten thousand dollars she was remarkably calm. I stood watching her as she waited on customers in her grimy, fly-specked store. Short and fat, with a watermelon stomach, she waddled around serving three worried Puerto Rican women.

The store sold groceries, newspapers, cigarettes, toys, soft drinks, and dusty cellophane packages of everything from handkerchiefs to baby pants. Her entire inventory and furnishings probably wouldn't bring more than nine hundred dollars.

In this neighborhood customers bought two eggs, or four frankfurters, or a quarter pound of hamburger. When one of her customers was rich enough to buy a dozen eggs at once, Mrs. Perez probably sold them with sullen reluctance. They brought more sold one or two at a time.

I threw a quarter on the counter and lifted a bottle of orange soda from the rusty old ice chest. She glanced at me from time to time while she waited on the others, her flat face expressionless, her black eyes barely showing through slits of puffy flesh.

When the store was finally empty of customers

I said, "There seems to be a slight discrepancy in your account, Mrs. Perez." A bit of an understatement, that. If her account had any larger discrepancy she might qualify among the top lady thieves of the year.

"Yeah," she said, "but that's all straightened out with Mr. Cressett. Who are you, anyway?"

I showed her my identification. "I'm a special investigator for Consolidated. Telephone them if you like."

She rested her fat elbows on the counter and just stared at me.

"What have you done with our money, Mrs. Perez?"

She merely grunted and continued to stare at me.

"What happened to it?" I asked. "The ponies, the stock market, or a boyfriend?" I glanced around at the poorly stocked shelves. "You certainly haven't invested it in inventory."

A customer came in and asked for half a loaf of bread. She picked up a sharp butcher knife and sliced through the middle of a wrapped loaf of bread. She then popped it into a paper bag, the middle slice exposed. I stood waiting while the customer pondered her next purchase.

A nonpracticing guitar player and former freak trying to go partially straight, I work for a psychosomatic wreck named Berkeley H. Barnes. Barnes is a private investigator, and I guess you might call me one too since I'm licensed. Getting licensed was something of a problem. At the time I had shoulder-length hair, Abraham Lincoln side and chin whiskers, and a black mustache six inches wide. Barnes convinced me I was too conspicuous for anything but political work or narking, the kind of work he stays away from, having a prejudice against spying on kids. So like Samson I allowed my strength to be shorn. At twenty-five I'm not getting any younger, and the three hundred a week offered was fairly good bread. My hair is now collar-length in back, and my sideburns stop a good inch above my jawline. Sometimes I feel naked and weak.

Consolidated Money Orders Corporation is one of Barnes's best clients. Their money orders are sold in stores all over the country. The poorer the neighborhood, the more money orders they sell. Without bank checking accounts, the people in these neighborhoods depend upon money orders to pay installments on the television set, the dinette furniture, the washing machine, and anything else that costs too much to pay for out of a single week's wages. Because of the semipoverty of these neighborhoods, the storekeepers who sell Consolidated Money Orders are not always the best of financial risks. Consolidated expects, and makes provision for, a certain amount of embezzlement. During a good week one of these storekeeper agents can get into Consolidated for five to ten thousand dollars. Then the computers catch on. Red lights flash, bells ring, and clerks scurry over to push the panic button.

Consolidated seldom prosecutes an embezzler. To prosecute generally means to lose all the money stolen from the company. The law doesn't give much help in pushing restitution. Of course, if an embezzler tries to pay back part or all of the money, the judge may be a bit more lenient in his sentence, but this is about as far as it goes. Usually, though, it is a complete loss for the company. When he is arrested the embezzler loses his business and thus has no income to use in paying back what he has stolen.

Instead of prosecuting, the company prefers to use the unspoken threat of prosecution as a lever to recover as much of the stolen money as possible. But the law, hair-splitting as usual, takes a sticky attitude. If you admit, for instance, that the storekeeper has embezzled from you, and fail to report this to the police, you are, in theory, concealing a felony. Theoretically you could be prosecuted yourself. In practice, the law tends to look the other way.

Ordinarily Consolidated handles its own embezzlement cases. When they have a funny one, they call us in. Mrs. Perez's case was in this category.

I had finished about half of the orange soda when the customer finally completed her shopping, adding five slices of ham and a can of baked beans to the half loaf of bread.

"What do you plan to do about our missing funds, Mrs. Perez?" I asked.

"I settled everything with Cressett," she said.

"You haven't settled anything with Cressett. The case is out of his hands."

She turned away. "Go screw yourself," she said. "Talk to Cressett. I ain't talking to *you*."

"Perhaps you'd prefer to talk to a man from the district attorney's office," I said, and went on to give the little speech that covers us, we hope, from the crime of compounding a felony. "Our money seems to be missing. It could be embezzlement. If you won't cooperate we shall probably have to get the police in and have a thorough investigation."

She swung around to face me again, her face showing some angry animation for the first time. "I signed a promissory note for Cressett," she said. "And now you got no right to prosecute me."

Very cute. Consolidated had entered into a debtor-creditor relationship with her and thus could not prosecute. "Do you have a copy of that note?" I asked.

"Yes."

"Let me see it."

She waddled to the back of the store for a moment and then returned with the note. She threw it on the counter in front of me.

I picked it up with a show of skepticism. I glanced at it, stepped back from the counter, ripped the paper in two, and stuffed the pieces in my pocket. "We can't accept your promissory note, Mrs. Perez," I said. It was a nasty trick, but if she and Cressett were in collusion to defraud Consolidated, why should I play straight with a couple of crooks?

Her pasty face turned shrimp-pink. She gripped the edge of the counter and yelled, "You lousy sonnafabitchin bastard!"

"Now maybe you'd like to tell me what you're going to do about our money," I said.

"Ed!" she screamed. "Ed, come out here!"

Ed looked like a professional wrestler with the heaves. He hadn't shaved in several days, and even though I am six one, he was taller and outweighed me, I estimated, by at least fifty pounds. He walked out to my side of the counter, his slack mouth open, panting asthmatically. "S'matter, Serena?" he asked in between pants.

"This lousy mother just stole my note from Consolidated so he can put me in jail!" She pounded the counter with her fat fists in outraged frustration. "Don't let him leave the store! Make him give it back!"

He moved over between me and the door. "What's that he done, Serena?" he panted.

"He stole my paper. Make him give it back!"

He stared at me. "You too cheap to buy your own paper, bud?" he asked.

By now she was waving her fat arms around frantically. "Oh you dumb pig!" she yelled. "It's the promissory note from Consolidated he took. He's got it in his pocket."

A glimmer of light began to seep through his mashed-up face. "You'd better give me that paper, mister," he said.

I picked up the soda bottle. I was armed, he wasn't. "Get out of my way, you slob," I said. "I'm leaving."

He moved back a step and brought up his fists like a professional fighter. They looked like two wrinkled, dried-up grapefruit. "No," he said. "No, you ain't leaving at all, sport."

"I'll crack the neck off this bottle and cut your face to ribbons," I said. I talk a good fight. Saves wear and tear on my big blue eyes. Surprising too how often a good bluff works. But this wasn't going to be one of those times.

He jabbed threateningly with his left. "Cough it up, sonny, before I separate your head from your neck," he said.

"Stand aside or you'll go to jail with your girl friend," I said, not believing for a second that he cared. When disaster strikes, keep talking.

The left was coming again, this time with serious intent. I jerked my head to one side, but not fast enough. It caught me a glancing blow on the cheek and was hard enough to start what brains I have buzzing like an electric razor.

I hopped back, shifting my grasp to the neck of the bottle. "Last warning," I said, drawing it back like Ashe getting ready to serve.

He tucked his chin down on his chest and lashed out at me again with the left. I was still backing up when it landed, but it was quite a jolt. Stopped the buzzing in my head, though. It changed to sheer pain. I brought the bottle down in a cannonball serve, aiming for the top of his head. It connected with the kind of satisfying thud that occurs when you walk into a door in the dark. Surprisingly, it didn't break.

He dropped down on one knee, waiting for the count.

"Two, three, four," I said loudly, waltzing stiffly toward the door. "Five, six," and I was through it and out on the street.

My right arm was soaked to the elbow, the remainder of the orange soda having drained down my sleeve. I walked hurriedly away, shaking my arm and dripping orange soda.

The whole incident had been startling. We never have violence from embezzlers. They are usually frightened, gentle little guys who had a moment of madness at Aqueduct. Facing prison, they hustle around and borrow several thousand from Uncle Joe or Cousin Max. If they can come up with one third to one half of the embezzled amount, Consolidated will generally accept a note for the rest, allowing them to pay it off by the month.

To let Mrs. Perez sign a note without any payment was strictly peculiar. Consolidated almost never lets anyone off the hook without partial payment, and in the rare cases in which they do the decision is made by Ryan, the general manager in charge of the New York operation. If Ryan had made such a decision, he wouldn't have asked Barnes to investigate, and Barnes wouldn't have sent me out to get my brains shaken loose and my topcoat and suit wrecked with orange soda.

I put a good four blocks between myself and Ed before looking for a pay telephone. By now he might be hearing "Nine!"

After the usual hassle and two dimes embezzled from me by the telephone company, I finally got through to Consolidated.

"This is Larry Howe," I said. "Let me speak to Mr. Barnes. He's probably with Mr. Ryan."

Barnes came on quickly. "Yes, Larry," he said.

"I'm calling from a pay phone four blocks from the Perez store," I said. "The situation *is* very peculiar. She claims Cressett allowed her to sign a note for the whole amount. I have her copy of the note. I have no further information. I have been hit in the head twice and drenched with orange soda."

"Orange soda?"

17

"She has a very tough friend named Ed."

"You have *her* copy of the note?"

"Yes." I leaned on my wet elbow and waited while he talked to someone else, Ryan probably.

In a moment he came back on. "Larry, Cressett is due back here for a meeting at eight o'clock. Why don't you grab a bite, do whatever is necessary to do with regard to the orange soda, and be back here at that time?" He was probably smiling. Barnes rarely laughs. There are too many things in the world that worry him.

"Okay," I said, and replaced the telephone, which was now about as sticky as my hand.

It was six-fifteen, and my two-room pad in the East Seventies was only a short subway ride away. It's comfortable and well managed. The exterminator comes regularly, once a month.

Shedding my wet coat and jacket, I went into the bathroom to examine my wounds. There was a slight abrasion on my jaw, and noticeable puffiness and bruising in the vicinity of my right sideburn. I moved my tongue around the inside of my mouth. Teeth all snug and tight.

I decided to put a pizza in the oven while I showered. An anchovy pizza. A gourmet's delight. Among poor gourmets, that is. I dug a pizza out of the freezer compartment of my refrigerator, opened a can of anchovies and spread them carefully on the top, popped it in the oven, and headed back to the bathroom. I like a good steaming soaking, and I don't top it

18

off with ice water, either. I think there may be something peculiar about people who take ice-cold showers.

The pizza was tasty, and the bottle of beer that accompanied it was all right. Wet. I was just finishing it when Desolate Deirdre dropped by to complain about the quality of some eggs she had borrowed from me. She comes from a small town in the South and does not understand that there is not a fresh egg to be had in all of New York. It's only the degree of nonfreshness that should concern you, I explained to her.

"Now, if the smell is overpowering—"

"The smell was overpowering, Larry," she said. "Those eggs were just plain rotten."

"I'll complain to the supermarket," I said, glancing at my watch. Seven-fifteen.

Deirdre is a handsome brunette of average size and shape. I use the word *handsome* because there is something definitely unfeminine about her. She has all the right feminine equipment; small waist, big hips, reasonably adequate bust, nice legs, but somehow...Maybe it's just the direct way she looks you square in the eye and complains about the eggs being rotten. Odd, too, because most Southern girls overdo the femininity thing.

In that little town she comes from they haven't even accepted sex, much less the sexual revolution. Deirdre has heard all about the rotten things that are going on in New York, and she's

19

glad she met an honorable, kind, clean-cut, decent man like me that she can trust, and not some dope addict.

Unfortunately, long before I met Isabel, the true-blue hangup of my life, Deirdre and I "went too far," as she put it. I don't think I'll ever hear the end of it. It's giving me an anxiety neurosis. Isabel may pop in sometime when Deirdre is there complaining, and our relationship may be tarnished with mistrust.

"You're all dressed up for a date, aren't you?"

"No, just a business appointment," I said.

"I must seem incredibly cheap to you after what happened," she said.

I sighed inwardly. "Not at all, not at all."

"You have no respect for me any more."

"That's not true. I've tremendous respect for you."

"We lost our heads."

"That's right. But believe me, I respect you."

We argued some more about her character, and whether it had really been cheapened or not, until I noticed that it was seven-thirty. I hustled her out, slipped on a topcoat that didn't have orange soda in the sleeve, hurried to the street, and grabbed a cab headed downtown.

Consolidated's midtown office occupies what was an old mansion on East Thirty-seventh Street. Completely converted, it is now a compact little five-story office building. National headquarters of the firm are in the Wall Street district. Thirty-seventh Street handles New York metropolitan area operations.

The anchovy pizza had left me with a monumental thirst. I stopped at the Coke machine on the second floor, but found the coin slot covered with adhesive and a small "out of order" sign taped to the front. My thirst would have to wait.

Barnes and Ryan were alone in Ryan's office. Barnes was rubbing his forehead, which is a bad sign. I found the small plastic container of Bufferin in my left trouser pocket, flipped it open, gave him two, and watched, mentally sucking a lemon, while he chewed them up without water. Barnes is in his forties, tall and skinny, about six foot three, with a rugged, tight-skinned face, gray eyes, and a sizable beak of a thin nose. He's also the biggest hypochondriac I've ever encountered. One of my jobs is to be his walking home medical adviser. My pockets bulge with medications designed to meet frequent health emergencies.

"My head was beginning to throb," said Barnes, "here." He pointed to the section immediately above his right eye.

I had arrived just in time. Let a headache really get going and he starts pounding his head with the heel of his palm and making a big scene.

"Berk says you got doused with orange soda," said Ryan, smirking. Ryan is vice-president in charge of the metropolitan New York area, a big job. He is middle-aged, on the plump side, with a mustache and thinning dark hair, wears the latest in natty but conservative clothes, and frequently bugs me. Getting doused was the least of my problems. I had expected my bruises to get some notice, if not sympathy.

"Thanks," I said. "I get half murdered trying to protect the interests of Consolidated, and you think it's funny." I smiled; he was an important client.

Ryan frowned. "Sorry," he said. "You don't look in such bad shape. Any broken bones?"

Broken bones he wanted. "No," I said.

"Well, it's not funny, I assure you," said Ryan, "when somebody lets a dame like Perez get off the hook by signing a note."

I reached in my jacket pocket and found the note I had torn in two. I handed the pieces to Ryan.

He fitted them together and studied them briefly, then handed them to Barnes. "It's our form, all right."

"Another Douglas case?" I asked. Douglas had been involved in a similar situation, on a much larger scale. Like Cressett, he was a supervisor. He had conspired with the owner of a small department store. Between them they had taken Consolidated for about twenty-five thousand. For providing the handy promissory note, Douglas received half. It was alleged. Consolidated was never able to prove it. The department store owner had apparently been on the brink of bankruptcy anyway. He filed, and that was the end of Consolidated's twenty-five thousand. Also the end of Douglas, jobwise.

Barnes removed the tips of his fingers from his forehead and said, "Cressett maintains that he did not have Mrs. Perez sign a note."

That was a switch. Douglas had brazenly admitted to letting Martin, the department store owner, sign the note. He had been swayed, he maintained, by Martin's verbal assurance that the whole amount would be repaid within two weeks.

"I didn't press Cressett," said Ryan. "I wanted to see the actual copy of the note. And dammit, it's our form, all right." He stroked his big brown mustache idly. "Very strange." He picked up his phone and dialed on the intercom wire. "Bob, would you come in here, please," he said, and replaced the handset thoughtfully.

Cressett was a well-built, muscular type, about thirty, I guessed. There was a clean-cut, American-boy openness about his face. All wide-eyed and innocent-looking. At the moment he was looking very puzzled.

"This is the copy of the note Mrs. Perez claims you had her sign," said Ryan, handing him the pieces.

He looked them over carefully, then shrugged. "It's our form, but damned if I understand it. I didn't give it to her."

Ryan stared at him. The atmosphere got so

cold I put my hands in my pockets. "Tell us exactly what happened when you saw Mrs. Perez," he said.

Cressett was a little flustered by the ice. "I—well, I gave her the usual story. I've always figured the place was a numbers drop, and so I figured, well, maybe we stood a good chance of recovery. At least five or six thousand, anyway."

"*Our* money orders sold in a numbers drop?" Ryan interrupted, his mustache bristling.

Cressett smiled apologetically. "Hell, Mr. Ryan, if we close out all our stores in Harlem we suspected of being numbers drops, we wouldn't have much business up there. That's the universal sport up there."

Ryan just grunted.

"I told her that if she could dig up six or seven thousand, we *might* let her sign a note for the rest and pay it off by the month. She said she thought she could borrow five thousand from her friend Juan. I said okay, but you'd better make it fast, because we get very nervous when we've been swindled, and we're practically ready to call the D.A."

Ryan grunted again.

"I did not have her sign any note," Cressett ended his speech slowly and emphatically.

Barnes, who had been listening carefully to Cressett, said, "Could someone there have slipped some forms from your attaché case while your attention was diverted?"

Cressett hunched his shoulder, turning to look at Barnes. "No. I didn't even have my attaché case with me."

'Did you have any promissory note forms with you?" asked Barnes.

Cressett nodded. "Yes. But in my inside jacket pocket." He reached inside his jacket and pulled out some folded forms. "These. And I didn't leave any with her."

"Somebody did," said Ryan.

"I'm sure I don't know who," said Cressett. "It sure wasn't me."

Barnes sighed. "At least we can check on whether it was typed here."

Cressett had placed the two pieces of Mrs. Perez's note on Ryan's desk. I bent over to look at them. The amount and the terms of repayment had been typed in. The carbon had even reproduced Mrs. Perez's signature.

"I wonder who has the original," I said.

"Good question," said Ryan. "With that floating around, we're in a ticklish spot."

"Someone here," said Barnes.

"Exactly," said Ryan.

Consolidated's building would be a little bit easier to get into than Fort Knox, but not much. The vault in the basement would have satisfied the most timid bank. It wasn't needed to protect the money from money order sales. Most stores banked the cash and paid Consolidated by check. But in addition to money order sales,

Consolidated operated an armored-car check-cashing service for industrial plants. Factories using the service paid their workers by check. From morning until late afternoon on payday, Consolidated's armored trucks would be on the grounds, teller's windows open on both sides, cashing these payroll checks for a fee. The night before a standard payday there could be well over a million dollars in Consolidated's midtown vault. Security arrangements were thus very tight. And while the promissory note forms would not be as rigidly accounted for as cash, you could not obtain them just by wandering into a supply room. They were kept locked in a bookkeeping safe in Ryan's office. The reps who served Consolidated's agents routinely would not have access to this type of form. A supervisor would. Ryan was still gazing at Cressett so glacially that his mustache was frosting over.

"Bob," he said, "I'm afraid I'm going to have to suspend you until this matter is clarified and resolved."

Cressett dipped his head slightly, tight-lipped. "I don't think that's very fair, Mr. Ryan. I didn't have her sign any note."

"Matter of policy," grunted Ryan. "There won't be any loss of pay if our investigation shows you had nothing to do with it."

Cressett stood up. "I think you ought to investigate *first,* before you tag a man with being a crook."

"Rules are rules," said Ryan. "Suspension doesn't mean we think you're guilty. There's an irregularity here to the tune of ten thousand dollars. Innocent or not, you're involved. I have no right to do anything but suspend you while the matter is being investigated."

Cressett clasped his hands behind his back. "Yeah. I know. But once you've been suspended, there's a sort of stigma that sticks."

Barnes had been studying Cressett's face. "Rod," he said, "why don't you let Bob take the day off tomorrow. Hold up at least a day on making it official. I'd like to have a talk with Mrs. Perez. Who knows, maybe something will come to light."

Ryan stroked his mustache while Cressett glanced at Barnes appreciatively. Ryan's first name is Roderick, believe it or not.

"I don't know, Berk," he said. "Oh hell, all right, we won't make it official. We'll review the situation tomorrow." He stood up and stretched. "Tomorrow's a big cee-cee day. I won't be able to spend much time with you on this, Berk," he said to Barnes.

By *cee-cee* he meant check cashing. Tomorrow was the fifteenth, one of the biggest payroll days, because it also happened to be a Friday.

Cressett had been edging toward the door. "Thanks, Mr. Ryan, Mr. Barnes," he said, his voice dropping as he went through the door before Ryan could change his mind.

"Larry and I will go back up there and try to talk to Mrs. Perez again. This evening," said Barnes.

I didn't care for that. "Hey, wait a minute," I said. "That goon may be pretty sore at me by this time. We better take a cop with us."

Ryan smiled. "Take Tip," he said. He turned on his intercom and said, "Ask Tipton to come in, will you please."

Flipping off the switch, he glanced at Barnes. "I'd prefer keeping the police out of this until we find out what happened to the original of that note," he said.

Tipton Horgan, known as Tip, Top, or Hot, was large and bulging with muscles. He was also the youngest supervisor at Consolidated. Barely out of college, where he had been boxing champion, he drove an eighteen-thousand-dollar Ferrari, lived in a tremendous mansion in New Canaan, all on twelve thousand a year. With the help of a very rich wife, most of us assumed. Why would anyone with inherited wealth bother with being a Consolidated supervisor?

Horgan glanced at Barnes and me and said, "What's up, folks? More skulduggery in the ranks of our sterling agents?"

Ryan explained our problem with Mrs. Perez. "Larry here got knocked around by her boyfriend. We decided reinforcements might be in order."

Horgan stroked his side whiskers thoughtfully. He had a reddish-brown fringe that extended down his jaw, across his chin, and up the other side. "Just because I happen to have developed a certain amount of expertise as a boxer, I am always being chosen for these strong-arm assignments. I'm a well-educated fellow with a high I.Q. and a great deal of talent as an actor. I want you to think of me as a man who can handle other situations than those merely requiring brute force." Ryan, who is not long on patience, was smiling and being very patient. "Tipton, I'm sorry if we're giving you the wrong impression. I see you as a man with a great future with this organization. If you don't want to go with Barnes, I'll assign someone else," he said.

Horgan held up one hand. "I wouldn't think of letting you down, Rod. Be glad to go."

There was the sound of a sneeze just outside the door, and David Gates, the New York manager, came in blowing his nose. A white-haired, pink-cheeked man in his sixties, he looked distraught.

"Finished inventorying the truck money?" asked Ryan.

"Yes, dammit." He folded his handkerchief and tucked it into his pocket. "The gee-dee time lock mechanism is jammed again, and she's locked in the *open* position."

Ryan muttered disgustedly. "I'll call Denzer," he said.

Gates kicked the leg of a chair around to face

29

him and sat down. "Probably be hours before they get here. They only have two night service men on call, and you know how long it takes when they start working on that monster of ours."

Ryan shrugged. "So you hold a couple of men for guard duty. It won't be the first time we've paid overtime for a temperamental time lock."

Gates nodded wearily. "I've asked Wicher and Hill to stay. What bothers me is that *I'll* have to be here until the wee hours too. Tomorrow's a tough enough day without being up all night too." He sneezed again and reached for his handkerchief.

"You getting a cold?" asked Ryan. "Anyway, there's no need for you to stay. I planned to be here for several hours to catch up on some work. I'll stay until the Denzer people are through and we're locked up tidy."

Gates looked relieved. "Heck, Rod, I hate to impose—"

"No imposition at all. I'm going to be here anyway."

Gates stood up. "I told Wicher and Hill to rotate. Two hours on and two off."

Ryan waved his hand negligently. "Don't worry. Get home and crawl into a hot whiskey toddy."

"Yeah," said Gates, smiling.

"No problem. Tom will be here too. Four of us

should be enough to keep an eye on things."
Tom was the regular night watchman.

Barnes, Horgan, and I moved toward the
door.

"Want me to call Denzer before I go?" asked
Gates.

"No," said Ryan. "I want to talk to them."

We slipped out while these nonconnected-to-
our-problem worries were being resolved.

As we headed through the foyer to the front
door John Wicher, a stocky, gray-haired man
wearing a uniform and holstered revolver,
stepped up to Barnes.

"A good evening to you, Mr. Barnes," he said.

Barnes stopped, smiling. "John, how've you
been?"

"Fair to middling. Old age creeping up on
me." Wicher reached into his jacket pocket. "Mr.
Barnes, would you mind signing my niece's autograph book? She collects celebrities." He handed
the small autograph book to Barnes awkwardly.

Barnes looked embarrassed. "I'm not a celeb-
rity, John." He accepted the book reluctantly,
and flipped through the pages, pretending interest. "FDR! Your niece goes back a ways."

Wicher smiled sheepishly. "Actually it's mine.
I'm going to leave it to her."

"I'd feel foolish, signing in the same book with
FDR."

"The *News* calls you 'New York's No. 1 Private
Eye.' "

"Even so—"

"One-thumb Fratinelli's in there."

Barnes laughed. "In that case—" He shrugged, then quickly signed and handed the book back.

"Thanks a million."

"Don't mention it. I'm flattered."

In the cab headed uptown, Barnes sneezed. "I'm probably catching his cold," he said, referring, I guess, to our brief encounter with Gates. I mentally reviewed my supply of remedies. Cold capsules would not do, because they had aspirin in them, and Barnes had already had ten grains of aspirin within the last half hour. Tranquilizer? Anticongestant? I settled on the placebo pills I carry which I understand are composed of flour and a little sugar.

"Here, take a couple of cold pills," I said. One day I would be arrested for practicing medicine without a license.

Barnes chewed them up gloomily. "They taste like flour," he said.

If I could just get him to swallow these things with water, like any normal person. "Probably what they use as a binder," I said. "You know, to hold the drug together."

"There's a sweetish taste too," he said, chewing. "Opium?"

"Probably," I said. "Don't worry about it. The thing to do is knock that cold out before it gets started."

Horgan, who had been slumped in the far corner of the cab, said, "You should take about five thousand milligrams of vitamin C."

I had enough problems without his putting his two cents' worth of medical advice in. "Massive doses of vitamin C do not work well with Mr. Barnes," I said, using a chilly but not downright unfriendly tone. "You know they have a drastic laxative effect upon certain people."

"Oh," said Horgan.

The cab driver, who had been listening, said, "The best thing to do for a cold—"

Barnes interrupted. "I don't want any more advice about what to do for a cold."

Hurt, the cab driver braked suddenly. "You mean I got no right to express an opinion? I mean, I'm just a cab driver. I'm too low on the social scale to have an opinion?"

Barnes made some unpleasantly hostile sounds. "Even if you were the President, I wouldn't want your opinion," he said.

"There's something about me personally?" asked the cab driver.

"Look," I said, "let's get going. We'll all be glad to hear what you should do for a cold."

The cab driver twisted around to look at me. "Well, what you do, you get laid. You work up a terrific sweat, then go out in zero weather and catch pneumonia. That the doctor can cure." He bent over and started to laugh, beating his fists on the curved top of the instrument panel.

I laughed dutifully at this old gag, Barnes muttered, and Horgan made hissing sounds. Eventually we continued on our way to Madam Perez's store, the cab driver still giggling.

"This we have to put up with *in addition* to a big raise in rates," muttered Barnes.

We filed into the dirty little store, Barnes leading the way. Ed was behind the counter, seated on a broken chair and looking as though he had a mean headache. He got up quickly when he saw me.

"Serena!" he yelled. "That son of a bitch is back again!"

He started around the counter to get me. Tip Horgan stepped in front of me and held up one hand. "I wouldn't, my friend, " he said. "You look dreadfully flabby."

Ed grabbed a wad of Horgan's shirt front and tried to jerk him aside. Horgan grasped his arm and pulled hard in the direction Ed was trying to move him, causing Ed to sit suddenly on the floor. *Sit* is a bit of an understatement. Actually he fell so hard he bounced at least twice.

Serena had come from the back and was now yelling. "I want you blanking motherblankers to get the hell out of my store!"

Obscenity of that type turns Barnes off. "Look here, madam," he said, "that kind of language only indicates a very poor vocabulary."

"You're a bunch of motherblanking crooks!"

34

she screamed. How about that? *We* were crooks.

"I don't like to hear a woman using this kind of language," Barnes said to me.

Ed got creakily to his feet and went back behind the counter. He recognized he was outnumbered, I guess.

"Mrs. Perez," said Barnes, "we have business to transact. I suggest we eliminate the noise and talk sensibly."

"I have nothing to say to you motherblankers."

Barnes winced. I think his generation is allergic to that particular obscenity, it involving incest and all.

"Mr. Cressett states that he did *not* allow you to sign a promissory note. I want to know where you got that note," said Barnes.

She put her elbows on the counter and stared at him sullenly. "Cressett is a motherblanking liar."

"Do you have a friend named Juan?" asked Barnes.

Her eyes flicked to me for a second and then back to Barnes. "Yeah."

"Would he lend you money to pay off part of this, ah, misunderstanding?"

"He might."

"This is what you stated to Mr. Cressett, isn't it?"

She started to reply, then shut her mouth tightly.

"Did you pay Cressett to let you sign the note?"

"I got nothin' more to say to you mother-blankers."

"How much did you pay off?"

"Get out of my store."

"It would seem to be our store, like," I said, "like we bought it for about ten thousand dollars."

She glanced at me. "You shut your motherblanking mouth, Junior."

That hurt.

Barnes sighed. "All this name-calling isn't getting us anywhere. I suppose we'll have to re-fer the whole thing to the district attorney's office."

She clenched her pudgy fists. "I've got witnesses that there was a promissory note signed. This crooked motherblanker stole it from me, but I still got witnesses."

"Madam, at best the promissory note was ille-gal collusion between you and possibly some em-ployee of Consolidated. I can't see what good your witnesses are going to do you. Whoever ac-cepted the note had no authority to do so," said Barnes.

She bared some very yellow teeth. "So sue me, you motherblanker!" She pointed at me. "This motherblanker comes in here and attacks me and takes the note away by force. Then he hits

Ed over the head with a soda bottle and fractures his skull!"

That was a lie. Laid on a railroad track, Ed's skull would derail a diesel.

"When I go into court and tell 'em what you done to me, you motherblankers, Consolidated's going to look like pig blank!"

Barnes turned and walked out of the store. We followed, with me keeping smartly ahead of Horgan.

"We aren't going to get anywhere with her until we have more information," Barnes said, yawning. "Let's call it a night."

It could be a sticky situation, public relations-wise. Barnes and Ryan would undoubtedly give it some serious thought. The idea of my attacking Mrs. Perez and beating up Ed might have some credibility in court. Back in my pad, I decided there was no point in worrying about it. I poured a can of beer and glanced through the papers, which I had had no time to read that morning. A young unmarried mother was quoted as saying, "Sex is of no importance to me. I was looking for a meaningful communication to fulfill a deep insecurity." This depressed me. I decided to go to bed.

The lighted dial of my electric alarm clock registered three-fifteen when the phone rang. And kept ringing. It could only be Barnes.

"Larry," he said, "meet me at Consolidated as quickly as you can get there."

"Yeah." I was half asleep.

"Are you awake? Listen, this is important."

"Sure. I'm awake."

"Consolidated has been robbed."

I told him I'd be right over.

Three police cars and an ambulance were double-parked in front of the Consolidated building. After about five minutes of stomping around in the cold with the cop at the door, I was finally admitted. Barnes and Ryan were downstairs, they told me.

The small lobby outside the steel grille partition was crowded. Two detectives were seated at a table taking a statement from Ryan. Three police technicians were fine-tooth-combing the area for dust, fingerprints, and other esoteric items. Two ambulance men were waiting to take away a blanketed figure on the floor. It gave me a chill to see that the blanket had been pulled over the face.

Barnes was standing off to one side, one hand cupped against his lower jaw. Barnes sometimes develops psychosomatic toothaches in times of stress.

I handed him a couple of Bufferin. "Who?" I asked, glancing at the figure on the floor.

He removed his palm and accepted the pills. "John Wicher, one of the guards. I just gave him my autograph."

"He's dead?"

Barnes nodded, looking sicker.

"How?"

"Blow on the head. Thin skull."

One of the detectives turned to look at us. It was Lieutenant Shunk, Barnes's old buddy from Homicide. Green-eyed, and with a face the texture of stale bread, Shunk is an original hardnose.

"Why don't you guys cut out the yakking and do something useful, like writing out individual statements covering your actions yesterday afternoon and evening?"

"I've given Lieutenant Shunk the full story on the Perez case," said Ryan, a little too hurriedly.

Shunk doesn't care much for private investigators. We had only tangled with him on a case once before, and he gave us a very hard time. Eventually he and Barnes developed some mutual respect. This occurred when Shunk found out about Barnes's work for the Anti-Cruelty to Animals Society. Barnes spends practically all his spare time with this be-kind-to-animals hangup. He's a director of the society, and being a lawyer as well as a private investigator, he handles a lot of their legal work free. This gave them something in common, because Shunk does love his dog. I figure it is because he couldn't possibly have any human friends.

Shunk hadn't missed Ryan's nervous remark. He said, "Yeah, Berk, you can tell the whole truth. We're not interested in your hanky-panky with that crappy little embezzlement case. This is murder."

"There's no hanky-panky," said Barnes. "Where can we go to write our statements?"

"Use my office," said Ryan.

I yawned. Not from boredom, but from sheer lack of sleep. Since Barnes had found out that I could type, I knew I'd have to do both statements. The thought made me very sleepy. I learned to type in the Army. Having volunteered for Airborne, I was assigned to clerk-typist school. That's the way it goes. You volunteer to be a cook and end up in a bomb disposal unit. The Army doesn't want anybody doing anything he'd like to do.

On the way to Ryan's office I asked, "How much did they get?"

"More than a half million, apparently."

"Wow."

It had been a very slick, quiet robbery. And definitely an inside job, said Barnes. Ryan had been dozing in his office, waiting for the Denzer people to come and repair the time lock. Hill, the other guard, was having two hours off duty and had been dozing in the third-floor ladies' rest room, which had a couch. Tomlinson, the night watchman, was probably punching his clocks on the fourth and fifth floors. They had come in with keys, gone to the vault, cracked Wicher's thin skull, scooped up more than a half million dollars in bills of large denominations, then left by the front door, relocking it carefully. The whole operation, Ryan estimated, hadn't taken more than ten or fifteen minutes.

"Did Wicher put up any kind of a fight?" I asked.

"His pistol was out of its holster, but not fast enough, apparently. He seems to have been taken completely by surprise."

"It would be possible, coming in with keys." Barnes nodded.

"It sure narrows it down," I said. "I mean, how many sets would there be?"

"Only two. Ryan's and Gates's. There's a third set, but it is locked in General Ellsworth's personal safe deposit box."

General Ellsworth was chairman of the board and chief executive officer of Consolidated. Also majority stockholder. Also reputed to be worth close to one hundred million slices. Man, that's a lot of bread.

"So all they have to do is rush over and arrest Gates," I said.

"That would be a bit precipitate. Several of the supervisors have had custody of the keys at one time or another. Long enough to have duplicates made."

I groaned and settled in at Ryan's secretary's desk. I uncovered her typewriter. "Why don't you make notes on what you want covered in your statement, and I'll type it up," I said. Might as well volunteer; he'd ask me to anyway. After searching through several drawers full of hand cream, face cream, eye cream, Kleenex, plastic overshoes, manicuring materials, aspirin, and a paperback entitled *Pornography for All,* I found some typing paper. Busy girl.

I quickly typed up an account of my activities hour by hour, giving the full story of my visits to the establishment of Madam Perez, with no censoring of her delicate nuances of speech. It wouldn't shock Shunk. Had he been there he would have replied in terms that might even have made Madam Perez blush.

Barnes came back with a few scribbled notes. "You did more than *that* in all those hours," I said.

"I'm getting a buzzing in my ears," he said. "You can cover the periods we were together." He wandered back to Ryan's office, where I could hear him collapsing on Ryan's leather sofa.

With some faking here and there I managed to write a statement for Barnes to sign. Then I settled down to read *Pornography for All.* What else can you do at five o'clock in the morning?

Dawn brought Ryan and Shunk upstairs, with Ryan commenting unfavorably on my choice of literature. I mentioned that it was the only thing available.

"She thought it was a book that would help her take better pictures," said Ryan.

They went into Ryan's office and woke Barnes. I wondered if his ears were still buzzing.

One of the uniformed cops came up with a big bag loaded with containers of coffee and doughnuts. The greasy doughnuts would give Barnes a temporary case of acute indigestion, but who was I to deny him that pleasure?

We settled in Ryan's small conference room and opened the containers of coffee.

"I want this boy Cressett, and I want him fast," said Shunk. "He's not in his apartment. Where in the hell would he be, shacking up with a girl friend?" He stirred his coffee briskly, splashing it over the sides.

Ryan shook his head. "I have no idea about that."

"You think he's skedaddled, don't you?"

Ryan shrugged.

"Who else had access to the keys?" I asked.

"Only Tip Horgan and David Gates," said Barnes.

"I thought some of the other supervisors had—"

"Ordinarily yes," said Barnes, interrupting. "The locks were changed only four weeks ago. During that period Horgan and Cressett were the only supervisors who had possession of them to open up or lock up."

Something I hadn't known before, which Barnes explained, Consolidated changed the locks every six months, routinely.

"I wouldn't want to make any accusations," said Ryan, "and I can't imagine Bob Cressett being involved in anything like this. On the other hand, I know goddamned well Dave Gates and Tip Horgan would *never* be involved in a deal like this. *No way*."

It seemed to me that there were other alternatives. "Suppose someone stole the keys for say a couple of hours, had duplicates made, then returned them to Cressett, Gates or Horgan without their even knowing the keys were missing?"

"How?" asked Ryan.

I shrugged. "Say Cressett has a girl friend. Suppose she took impressions of the keys while he was asleep?"

Shunk slurped some of his coffee noisily. "Goddamned stuff is hot enough to melt your goddamned fillings."

Ryan said, "The time lock isn't easy to set. If you do it wrong, it begins to howl electronically, both at Denzer and at the precinct. You can get it locked into orbit either way though. It doesn't have enough brains to know whether the vault door is open or closed. But getting it set properly takes some special know-how."

He had a point. The only way an outsider could have carried out this tricky job would have been through an accomplice, one of the tellers counting the truck cash, or one of the guards. And one of these men fiddling with the time lock would be immediately suspect. Nor would he find any privacy. Consolidated's rules required there to be more than two people present when the vault was open. On the other hand, if one of the tellers saw Gates, Horgan, or Cressett fiddling with the time lock he would think nothing of it.

As it turned out, no one saw anyone setting the time lock. The men counting and packaging money in the vault were too busy shuffling and itemizing the green stuff.

But the question everyone wanted answered was, Where was Cressett?

2

During the next two days Barnes and I got very little sleep. Ryan approved an all-out attack. "Don't spare any expense, Barnes," he had said, mopping his brow with a damp handkerchief. "I want that son of a bitch caught before he spends any of our dough. He could blow it in Las Vegas in a week!" It wasn't so much the five hundred thousand dollars that teed him off. Each executive employee was bonded for two hundred and fifty thousand dollars, and Wickersham of England also provided full coverage for armed robbery or burglary. The bonding company would pay half, and Wickersham would pay the other half. But. Following a loss of that size, insurance premiums would skyrocket. Consolidated, with offices in one hundred and ten cities, would be paying out almost as much in increased premiums as the loss. Every year. You don't mess with those insurance companies, man.

To beef up his staff, Barnes called in all three of the freelancers he used from time to time, Tony Wilson, Harry Weiner, and Bill Perkes.

All were pros and pretty competent. Tony Wilson had a drinking problem, but usually managed to keep sober for a week or so when Barnes needed him. Weiner and Perkes were retired cops, detectives actually, and knew the crime scene in the five boroughs like an actor who has been in the same play for seven years.

Shunk, of course, had turned a lot of his men on to the problem too. General Ellsworth had one or two friends at City Hall.

But with all this talent, Cressett had done an efficient disappearing act, and immediately, at least, there was no trace. His apartment was only three blocks from Consolidated's midtown office, and he had customarily kept his car in Consolidated's parking lot, which was in the back of the converted town house and extended through to the next street. The car was missing. Cressett was missing. Nothing seemed to be missing from his apartment, however, indicating his departure had been hasty and unplanned. Razor, toothbrush, and all other personal articles remained undisturbed in his bathroom and bedroom.

Barnes had taken over the personnel records and had put Wilson, Perkes, and Weiner to work checking out all relatives, friends, and other contacts close to Cressett. He put me to work on David Gates, and took over the file on

Tipton Horgan himself. This brought us a squawk from Ryan.

He came thumping into the conference room looking irritated. "Why are you wasting time on Gates and Tip? They have about as much chance of being involved as Norman Vincent Peale."

Barnes gets very edgy when anyone tries to tell him how to run his business. "I have three very good men tracking Cressett," he said, "and I'm sure Shunk has at least ten doing the same thing." He gave Ryan a long, raised-eyebrow stare.

Ryan cold-stared him back. "*You* are the head man," he said. "*You* should assign *yourself* to a priority like Cressett."

Barnes consulted his cigarette notebook. He allows himself ten filter-tips a day, and religiously notes every cigarette smoked and the time, like, "No. 3, 11:36 A.M." He now made a careful entry. "Rod, you're a very good client, and I value your friendship," he said, tucking the small book away and reaching for his cigarettes. "But you'll have to let me handle this in my own way. Or get someone else."

A flicker of anger crossed Ryan's face, then slight embarrassment settled in. "Well," he said, "of course there are things you don't understand. I don't know just how to put this, but—" Barnes fondled his cigarette lovingly like a gourmet turning a truffle. "But what?"

49

"But you'd better be damned careful about any inquiries you make about Tip Horgan."

"Why?"

Ryan hesitated. "This is very confidential, understand. It's a well-guarded secret here, as the saying goes, but Tip is General Ellsworth's grandson. He's just learning the business from the ground up, so to speak."

"Oh."

"He'll be president of Consolidated one day. And, as you know, there's already so much money in the family that a half million dollars, well, hell, what's a half million dollars to them?"

Barnes lit his cigarette. "Don't downgrade a half million dollars. It's a respectable sum, even to a multimillionaire."

Ryan shook his head. "I wouldn't want to be in your shoes, or mine, if it got back to the General that you were making inquiries about Tip, as though he might be a common criminal."

Barnes smiled. "I'll be very discreet. Anything I do will be handled personally. Rod, I don't suspect Tip, but let me point out that it wouldn't be the first time a scion of the very rich got into a jam and had to get his hands on a lot of liquid cash in a hurry."

Ryan grunted. "I strongly advise you to stay off Tip's back."

I said, "Remember that guy, what's-his-name, who tried to corner one of the commodity markets? Every time the price fell one point, he was on the hook for sixteen million dollars."

Ryan gave me a cold stare. "I think I can safely assure you that Tip is not speculating in the commodity market."

We were interrupted by Shunk, who came in looking irritated, which is the way he generally looks.

"Any progress on locating Cressett?" asked Ryan.

Shunk pulled one of the conference room chairs out and sat down heavily. "Some," he said. "We've located his girl friend's sister. Now all we have to do is locate his girl friend. I suspect she's with Cressett."

Ryan brightened. "Great."

"Not so great," said Shunk. "We haven't been able to uncover any information on the girl, other than her name, which is Joyce Richards. We can't even find out where she lived before she skedaddled with Cressett, if she did indeed skedaddle with Cressett."

"Can't the sister help you?" asked Barnes.

"No. Can't or won't. I suspect won't."

"Why?"

"Cop hater."

Shunk stared at me, rubbing his chin thoughtfully. "Which brings me to the purpose of my visit. This Pamela Richards, the sister, is only twenty-three. I'm just thinking out loud, but suppose we sicked some personable young guy, like Larry here, on her. I mean, he manages to meet her, gets to know her, has no connection with the police. You see what I mean."

Barnes nodded. I nodded. When a guy like Shunk refers to you as "personable" you must be doing something right.

"I mean," said Shunk, "this chick doesn't have too many brains, and she might let something slip to Larry, seeing as how there's bound to be a certain amount of simpatico when two nits get together."

"Thanks," I said.

"I don't think you're being fair to Larry," said Barnes. "He has his intellectual side."

Shunk barked. It may have been a laugh. "Don't mind me, Larry, just friendly needling."

That was a lie. As I said before, the only friend Shunk has is his dog, and personally I question the dog's intelligence.

"Where do I find her?"

He scribbled an address on his note pad and tore it off. "Lives on Sutton Place," he said, handing it to me.

"Rich?"

He barked again. "Let's say the young lady is a very successful businesswoman."

"What does she do?"

Shunk smirked. "I don't know whether you can call a chick who charges a thousand dollars a trick a whore, but that's what she does."

"A thousand dollars!"

"Maybe she ought to be called, like, a courtesan. I mean, for that kind of dough."

"A thousand dollars!"

"I don't believe it," said Ryan.

"S'truth. The boys in Vice know about her, but her clients carry so much clout, well, you know how it is. Even the I.R.S. is afraid of her."

"I find this very hard to believe," said Ryan.

"Is this on expense account?" I asked.

"No!" yelled Ryan.

Barnes said, "If you were just another customer, chances are she wouldn't confide in you. Not for a while anyway, longer than we want to take."

Okay. Make it hard for me. "What makes you think I can establish that kind of rapport fast without throwing money around?"

"Money she's got plenty of. From rich old men," said Shunk.

Tightwads. Penny pinchers. My best suit was in the cleaners, too. "Okay," I said. "You realize that I may rub her the wrong way. We may not even get friendly."

Shunk barked some more. "We don't want you to rub her, just talk to her."

I picked up the conference room telephone and called my friend Freeman Crockley, who sells encyclopedias. That is, he goes out and sells a set whenever he runs out of bread, which is, say, two or three times a week.

"Freeman," I said, "I want to borrow your sales kit for a few hours. Okay?"

"Why do you want it?"

"I want to see if I can sell an encyclopedia. Don't worry, I'll credit you with the commission if I do."

"There's a twenty-five-dollar deposit on the kit." Trusting.

"I'll pay it."

"If you return it in good shape, you can have the bread back. I don't know what you want it for, but this selling bit sounds far out. I mean, man, you're making plenty of bread without *that*."

Out of the corner of my eye I could see that Barnes was staring at Shunk with a pleased smile. Shunk wasn't impressed. "He'll get his ass thrown right out of there. That chick has about as much interest in encyclopedias as I have in astrology."

"Don't be too sure of that," said Barnes.

As I replaced the handset, Shunk said, "Why don't you go as an Avon Lady?" Then he barked three times, it was so funny.

I grabbed a cab to Freeman's pad, left my twenty-five, and collected his kit, which weighed about fifty pounds, then went on to my own pad to don some thrilling threads. Pink tweed jacket, red and yellow striped shirt, electric-blue tie with orange stars, dark-blue bell-bottoms with white stripes, two-tone red shoes.

54

Pamela Richards' apartment was in a small building without a doorman or reception desk. I pushed the button next to her copper engraved nameplate. A very nice voice asked, "Who is it?"

"Larry Howe. There's a very urgent matter I wish to discuss with you."

"Harry?" asked the voice. The lock clicked open and I walked in and up to the third floor, since the buzzer had been labeled "3-B." I let the knocker fall a couple of times. The door opened and before me stood one of the most beautiful chicks I have ever encountered.

She looked at me with a surprised expression. "I'm sorry," she said pleasantly, "I don't believe I know you. I thought you were Harry."

"Larry Howe," I said, breathing hard. "Larry Howe."

She had a high, smooth forehead, and her hair was gold with a subtle hint of red in it. Her eyes were widely spaced, light brown, almond-shaped, and tilting just a fraction toward her nose, but not enough to give her an Oriental appearance. It was an intelligent, alert face, with a promise of a sense of humor in the mouth, which was just the right size, not too large and not too small. She really turned me on. Lights flashing, bells ringing. I forgot why I was there.

"Well," she said, glancing down at my sales kit, "what is it? Are you selling something?"

"I, uh—"

"What are you selling?"

What *was* I selling? I jiggled the case thought
fully. "Encyclopedias!" I yelled.

She smiled at my obvious confusion. "Is it a
good encyclopedia?"

"Of course. I wouldn't sell anything but the
best."

She just stood there looking at me, smiling.

"May I step in and tell you a bit about *Knowledge Unlimited*?"

She hesitated, but then opened the door wider
and motioned me in. Her living room was large
and expensively furnished, with great floor-to-
ceiling windows overlooking the East River. She
strolled over to one of the large sofas, sat in one
corner, and reached for a cigarette. I lit it for
her, then placed the sales kit on the sofa between
us and sat down.

I opened the case and began to sort out the
materials. Confident of my ability to ad lib, I had
not looked at them earlier. There was a sample
volume, BOI to CRE, a raft of folders, order
pads outlining time-payment terms, ballpoint
pens stamped *Knowledge Unlimited* in gold, and a
dictionary. I spread out one of the accordion
folders.

"Here," I said, "is *Knowledge Unlimited*. Twenty-four big volumes, more than twenty-five thousand pages, more than thirty million words, most
of them English!"

"What does it cost?"

"Wait," I said, "don't even think about the cost. The cost is inconsequential. When you buy *Knowledge Unlimited* you are buying a massive reservoir of intellectual stimulation, a cultural treasure that will last a lifetime."

She relaxed against the back of the sofa and stared at me. "You're a funny kind of a salesman."

"That's what the sales manager keeps telling me."

The phone rang. She got up. "Excuse me," she said, and walked over to an opened secretary near the other end of the room, sat down, and picked up the phone.

"Fenton! How nice of you to call."

There was a pause while she sat idly kicking the edge of the secretary with one beautifully sandaled foot. "The diamond pin was simply gorgeous. I mean, I had it appraised. I must admit, Fenton, I was startled. You really shouldn't have." There was another pause while she listened. "Fenton, before I accept it, I'd like to get one thing clear. It won't change our relationship. I mean, I can't credit it against—you know, it would just become too confusing doing things that way."

I studied the sample volume, my heart breaking. Pamela, Pamela, how could you?

"Tomorrow at four? Let me check." She glanced at her opened diary. "That will be fine. Look forward to seeing you. And thanks again so much for the beautiful gift. I'll think of you every time I wear it."

She replaced the phone and came back to the sofa. "Now, where were we?"

I flipped the sample volume. "Think of the pleasure of browsing through these volumes, of astounding your friends with scintillating talk gleaned from these stimulating pages."

She wrinkled her very pretty nose in a way that indicated she wasn't impressed.

"What are your special interests? The theater, dancing, poetry, motion pictures, bicycle racing?"

She smiled at the bicycle racing. "I've always been very interested in the theater. I've had some small parts in off-Broadway productions."

Of course. She would be. "THEA, that would be in volume 20, which unfortunately I do not have with me. Pick something between BOI and CRE."

"Bee-oh-eye?"

"Here, BOI. How about BOYS? Are you interested in boys?"

"Not particularly. I think older men are more interesting."

I flipped the pages desperately. "Here's BOILING POINT and, oh, here's BOILING ALIVE. Say, did you know that they used to execute people in England by boiling them alive? Repealed in 1547."

She shook her head.

"How about CARNIVOROUS PLANTS, or here, look, BURIAL—"

She stood up.

I closed the book. "I'm sorry. I know if I had the THEA volume you'd love the article on the theater. It tells everything you want to know and a lot more besides. Tell me about the parts you had off Broadway."

She stood looking at me. "Would you like a drink or a cup of coffee or something? I mean, you seem sort of rattled. I mean, are you always this nervous?"

"Coffee would be great." One drink and I might start babbling, "I love you. Give up this cynical, promiscuous life and fly with me to Kansas to start all over."

Over coffee she told me that she had had enough small parts to decide she was no actress. We chatted for a while about the theater, on, off, and off-off Broadway.

"Are you from a large family? Lots of brothers and sisters?" I asked.

"One sister."

"Is she as beautiful as you are?"

"How can I answer a question like that?"

"You don't like your sister."

"Why do you say that?" She sipped her coffee. "Though it's true."

"Is your sister an actress too?"

"She tried."

"Married and settled down with six kids, I'll bet."

"No. Actually she's still trying. Gets a modeling assignment once in a while."

I finished my coffee. "I'll bet she works for the Plymouth Agency. Every model I've ever met works for Plymouth."

She was beginning to look bored. "I wouldn't know. We don't see each other very often."

The phone rang and she excused herself again. "Horace! How sweet of you to call."

Well, it was a beginning. Check the model agencies. Of course, there were eight million model agencies.

"Tomorrow at eight? Just a sec. Okay. Look forward to seeing you."

I shuddered. Already she was making two thousand dollars tomorrow. If she averaged one date a day, that was three hundred and sixty-five thousand dollars a year, plus diamond pins with startling appraisals. It was all wrong, like paying five thousand dollars for a bottle of 1848 wine. It couldn't possibly be worth that much.

She returned to the sofa. "Now, where were we? You're supposed to be selling me a set of *Knowledge Unlimited,* and you won't even tell me what the price is. Actually, I've been hearing their television advertising and I'm sort of half-way interested in owning a set."

I shuffled through the order forms. "The imitation-leather-bound set is $249.98, and the genuine Moroccan-leather set is $339.98. You can buy them outright or on time."

She took one of the brochures and studied it for a while. "You didn't mention about the free dictionary I'm supposed to get, and the ballpoint pen. I get the pen just for talking to you."

I handed her a pen. "I'm glad you brought that up. This is a sample of the dictionary. It is one of the weightiest dictionaries I have ever carried. And it's literally jam-packed with words. If you find a wordier dictionary on the market, write us about it."

She smiled. "I don't see how you sell anything, kidding around the way you do. If it wasn't for what they said on television, I'd never be buying this set."

I let my face fall and tried to look hurt.

"Oh, now I've made you feel bad. But really, for your own good, you ought to concentrate more on telling people about the advantages of the set, and why they should buy it."

I smiled sadly. "You're right. I guess I've just been trying to show off."

"You're a clean-cut, good-looking fellow, and you speak beautifully. You could double your income if you worked harder at it. I mean, sort of quit fooling around. And you should dress more conservatively. I mean, I think your clothes are cute, but a lot of people, they'll take a look at you and say, 'This encyclopedia can't be very stable or authoritative when it's sold by a man wearing a pink tweed jacket and a blue tie with orange stars."

I nodded slowly. She was absolutely right.

The phone rang again and she left me to answer it. Her broker this time. She slipped on a pair of heavy, black-framed glasses and began reading her list in the only slightly interested tones of a housewife giving her order to Gristede's. "Sell a hundred shares of," and her voice would drop, "buy five hundred of mumble-mumble, get rid of *all* of my murmur murmur, and, oh, buy a hundred shares of IBM."

A hundred shares of IBM? Forty thousand dollars?

After she finished, she picked up her checkbook and scribbled in it.

She came over and handed me the check. "I'll take the genuine-leather-bound set."

I held the check, fanning it to dry the ink. "You know, I hope you won't think I'm presuming, but, well I make twenty percent commission on each sale, and this is the first encyclopedia set I've sold. I appreciate all your good advice. It would make me very happy if you would let me take you to dinner."

From the doubt on her face I expected her to say no.

"At a good place. 21? Four Seasons?"

She smiled. "You made about sixty-eight dollars. Why should you spend all of it taking me to dinner? You'll never get ahead throwing your money around that way."

"What should I do with it?"

"Invest it in good stocks. Some excellent ones are very cheap right now."

I shook my head. "I'd rather take you to dinner."

She sank back on the sofa, exasperated. "You should learn to *save* your money, not throw it away."

"It's very important to me that you have dinner with me. If you don't have dinner with me I will give the entire sixty-eight dollars to charity."

"That's better than giving it to Four Seasons."

"*Okay.*"

She smiled at my faintly belligerent tone. "Look, if you must have dinner with me, we'll have it here. I don't want you to spend your whole commission taking me to dinner."

This wasn't getting us any closer to Joyce Richards, but who could tell? These things took time, and I was enjoying myself.

"At least let me buy a bottle of good wine."

She gave the matter some serious thought. "Okay. Get a bottle of Pouilly-Fuissé 1962. Everything was super that year except red Bordeaux."

She glanced at her watch. "It will go well with lobster tails. I have some lobster tails in the freezer."

Outside, I wondered if I should go home and

get my guitar. After all, Pamela and I *were* contemporaries. I decided against it. It was a little thick. Anyway, she probably listened to Mozart and *My Fair Lady* to keep in tune with her clients. This chick was dedicated to two things. Making money and putting other people on the right track for making money.

I called Barnes and told him that all I had so far was the model agency angle. They could begin checking them and maybe track down her address. Also that I was going back to have dinner with Pamela at seven.

"You, ah, didn't commit us for a thousand dollars?" he asked.

"Certainly not."

"Ryan was quite adamant on the subject."

"Don't worry. My only expenses so far are twenty-five dollars' deposit on the sales kit and a bottle of Pouilly-Fuissé 1962, whatever that costs."

"Pouilly-Fuissé 1962?"

"To go with the dinner she's going to prepare."

"She has invited *you* to dinner?"

He needn't have sounded so incredulous.

I went home, took a shower, put on a gray banker's pin stripe, blue shirt and black tie, black shoes. The man you are about to see, Pamela, could be working for Chase Manhattan.

Seven liquor stores later I found a bottle of Pouilly-Fuissé 1962. Wow. It was still less expensive than taking her to dinner. I got a receipt for it. Ryan would never believe it otherwise.

Her eyes narrowed when she saw my new uniform. "You're not the same person."

"You said I should dress more conservatively."

"I liked you better in the pink jacket."

"I'll go home and change."

She smiled. "If you're going to wear a blue shirt and a black tie, wear a light gray suit, not a dark gray suit. You look like a gangster."

What a fusspot. "How many gangsters do you know?"

I followed her into the kitchen and deposited the Pouilly-Fuissé carefully onto a table. She handed me an ice bucket.

"Make yourself a cocktail if you'd like. You'll find everything in the bar in the living room."

"Aren't you having any?"

"I never drink anything stronger than wine. You can pour me a Dubonnet on the rocks."

I had the feeling she was regretting her impetuosity in inviting me to dinner. The phone rang. She picked up the kitchen extension. "Maxwell! How darling of you to call." A silence, then, "No, I can't make it this evening. Okay, call me in a day or so."

I was costing her a thousand dollars, that's what. Maybe two thousand. Someone probably called while I was out.

"I have a feeling you're sorry you invited me to dinner. All these men calling you for dates.

You'd probably rather be with them," I said, putting on my best hurt look.

She came over and put her hands on my shoulders. "Larry! I hurt your feelings about the clothes, didn't I?" She kissed me on the cheek.

After that the situation got a little more friendly, but I wondered about making a pass at her. It would be sort of like stealing money right out of the bank.

The dinner was really great. This girl had the heart of a gourmet banker. We polished off the Pouilly-Fuissé, and it was worth every dollar Ryan was going to pay for it.

I snapped my fingers. "Joyce Richards. I used to know a girl named Joyce Richards. Is your sister's name Joyce?"

She frosted over. "When?"

"Oh, two or three years ago."

"Where?"

She had me there. Any further identification might land me right in the glue works.

"Come to think of it, it was Joyce *Richman*. She worked in an ad agency."

"Oh."

"What's the matter?"

"A detective was here this morning asking me about Joyce."

"Oh. Is she in trouble?"

"I wish I knew."

"Is there anything I can do to help?"

Some of the frost melted. She shook her head. "Joyce can take care of herself."

She just happened to have a couple of bottles of champagne in the refrigerator. Her record library had plenty of Beethoven, Mozart, and *My Fair Lady,* but also some good rock and folk rock albums. Incidentally, I dig Mozart, but we played rock, and drank champagne, and in between records we talked about our philosophies of life.

I'm a little fuzzy on it, but I gathered she planned to buy an island near Jackie and have a yacht bigger than theirs.

After we finished the second bottle of champagne, we started to play hide-and-go-seek. She would go hide and I would go seek her. That place had more damned closets. I think she had a thing about hiding in closets, and shrieking bloody murder when I found her. We wrestled through about six closets, the last one in her bedroom. She had one of these king-size beds about eight feet square. As we wrestled out of the closet, she broke away took a running dive onto the bed, a perfect half-jackknife. Five pillows shot up in the air and onto the floor. Holding my nose, I ran and jumped onto the bed.

There was a ripping noise, then a gurgling sound.

She sat up. "You've ruptured my water bed!"
"What?"

"Quick. There's a thousand gallons of water in this damned thing." She jumped up and ran to the kitchen.

I climbed out and looked. Sure enough, water was running out of a corner at the foot.

She came running back with two saucepans and a large casserole, and shoved the casserole pot under the leak. You'd never believe how fast those damned things filled up. As soon as one filled, I would grab it and run for the bathroom while she shoved another under the leak.

If you want to sober up in a hurry, forget about black coffee. Try emptying pots for a couple of hours.

"Don't you have anything bigger?" I puffed.

"If I go to look, they'll run over."

After about four hundred trips to the bathroom the flood subsided. The water bed had run dry. And I must say the white shag rug was pretty sodden. Like walking in the deepest Everglades. We put down all kinds of things, trying to blot it up. Towels, sheets, paper towels, rolls of toilet paper spun out as fast as we could unwind.

Finally we gave up, convinced we had done everything we could.

We went out to the living room. She sank down on the sofa and lit a cigarette. I tilted the champagne bottle hopefully. Empty.

"You destroyed my water bed," she said bitterly.

"It can be patched."

"I'll never feel safe in it again."

"Sorry."

"You jumped on it too hard. Why would any one jump on a water bed feet first?"

"That's the way I jump. Diving bothers my sinuses."

I was exhausted. I felt more like saying, "Just tell me for chrissake where your stupid sister Joyce is and I'll go home." I never worked so hard in my life to get *one* little bit of information. And not to even mention the frustration of having our game of hide-and-go-seek turn out so poorly.

"Listen," I said, "I want to tell you something. Your sister Joyce is in great danger. If she's with Bob Cressett, she can be arrested as an accomplice in a half-million-dollar robbery with murder. How would you like that, huh? Your sister sent up for murder."

It took a moment to penetrate. She was tired from moving all those pots around. "You're a lousy cop. Get the hell out of my apartment!"

"I'm not a cop. I'm a private investigator. I work for Consolidated Money Orders."

"Cop!"

"I'm not interested in putting Joyce in jail. Only in recovering the money. I couldn't care less about putting Joyce in jail."

"Get out!"

"Not until you listen to reason."

She jumped up and hurried out of the room. In about thirty seconds she was back, pointing a dainty little automatic at me.

"Get out of here, or I'll *kill* you. You came in here and deliberately ruptured my water bed."

I stared at her reproachfully. "Pamela! You could do that, after all the fun we had wrestling in those closets?"

"I'll shoot you right in the heart!"

I got up wearily. "All right, I'll go." On my way to the door I had to pass her. When I was about three feet away I made a quick dive, grabbed her arm and hoisted it skyward. The gun went off. The noise was hardly louder than the champagne corks we had been popping.

"Don't shoot again," I said, "you're messing up your ceiling." We glared at each other, eyeball to eyeball, her right hand extended high in the air, my left hand holding it up there. I put my right hand in the small of her back and said, "Care to dance?"

She started to giggle. I pulled her close. "You know," I said, "it's quite possible that I could help Joyce."

She quit giggling. "Ha."

We stood there for a while, locked in our nonamorous embrace.

"Do you mind if I put my arm down? It's going to sleep."

"Promise not to shoot any more holes in the ceiling?" I lowered her wrist, then gently disengaged the gun.

"All we want is the money," I said. "The cops can worry about Cressett. Help me get that message to Joyce. If it's possible to untangle her from this mess, I promise you I'll do everything in my power to keep her out of it."

She stared at me, still skeptical. "Joyce wouldn't have anything to do with robbery and murder."

"Why not?"

"She's a scaredy-cat. Always has been."

"If she's messing around with Cressett, she may be dragged into it, innocent or not. If the police catch her with him, and he has the money, she's certain to be tagged as an accomplice." That wasn't altogether true, but it was in a good cause.

"The whole thing's silly. Joyce wouldn't have the nerve to lift a thirty-nine-cent lipstick from Woolworth's."

I was still holding her tightly. "All the more reason to shake her loose from Cressett."

She raised her hand and pushed my shoulder. "Let me go."

I released my grip and stepped back.

"Well?"

"How do I know you're a private eye and not a cop?"

I showed her various pieces of identification, including my license.

"If I take you to Joyce, will you promise not to tell the cops?"

"Yes."

She put her hands on my shoulders and looked up into my eyes with her beautiful eyes. "And you promise you'll try to help her?"

"Yes. So help me, I swear I will."

"She works in a place called the Naked Owl."

3

It took some doing, but I finally managed to convince Pamela that it would be wise to bring Barnes with us. I argued that he packed a lot more weight, prestigewise, than I did, and that he could do a lot more to help Pamela, if she needed help, than I could. Which was true. A stronger reason, which I didn't mention, was that I didn't know what I was getting into. It could be a very delicate situation, or nothing. Joyce might not even be in touch with Cressett. If she was, Barnes's greater experience was most certainly called for. If I carried on alone, and blew it, we'd both be in big trouble with Shunk.

Telephoning Barnes at one-thirty in the morning gave me a certain amount of pleasure, since it woke him up. It was usually the other way around. After some hesitation, he agreed to keep Shunk out of it until we found out whether Joyce could lead us to Cressett. We arranged to meet in front of the Naked Owl.

We sat in the cab in front of the Naked Owl and waited for Barnes to arrive, listening to the meter ticking away Ryan's money cheerfully. After about two dollars' worth of waiting an-

73

other cab arrived, and Barnes unfolded his six-foot-three frame through the door.

Introductions were brief. I was afraid Pamela would demand a full identification ceremony, but apparently she had read about Barnes in the *Daily News*. Also as a distinguished-looking middle-aged man who wore three-hundred-dollar tailor-made suits, he could be a potential client. Anyway she greeted him with more warmth than was necessary.

Barnes had the bemused look he gets when dealing with good-looking women who can't be put into a particular niche. He surveyed her carefully from head to toe and said very little.

From the psychedelic decor I gathered that the Naked Owl had started out as a discotheque. But from the middle-aged, visiting firemen-type customers, it was apparent that it had become a typical nightclub-clip joint.

Inside we were met by a red-faced, mean-looking guy wearing slacks, an open sport shirt, and a green sports jacket.

"Table for three," I said.

He chewed his rubbery-looking lower lip for a few seconds. "Yeah, I guess I can take care of you."

He led us to a table located on the edge of the dance floor, then said loudly, "Don't forget to take care of the headwaiter, fellows."

"Okay," I said, "send him over."

His face got redder. "Whatta you, wise guy? *I'm* the headwaiter."

Some head waiter. "Sorry," I said, and fished out a five and handed it to him. He grunted his appreciation.

"What'll it be, folks? How about a bottle of champagne?" He was attempting to be genial, but it sounded like a snarl. Pamela and I looked at each other. We were still burping champagne, softly.

"Eeucch," she said.

"Scotch," said Barnes.

"My sister Joyce is in the show," said Pamela.

He grinned another big snarl. "That don't get you no discount, you know. You still got to order a drink, sweetie, and I ain't got all night."

"Dubonnet for her and Scotch on the rocks for me," I said hurriedly.

"What a crude type," said Pamela as he slouched off to turn our order over to one of the waiters.

The lights dimmed and spots focused on the dance floor. The M.C. walked on, dragging a beaten-up-looking old mike. It was the *headwaiter*. What a low-budget joint!

He began to tell some pretty stale jokes, pausing at each punch line for laughs. He got one here and there. Now I could understand why he was so bitter. He finally concluded by yelling, "All right you jerks, I'm gonna introduce

Francine and her snake, Tremont. And Tremont can't hurt ya, because you're already dead, ya bastards!" That got his biggest laugh.

After a roll of drums and fanfare from a single trumpet, Francine slithered out to the floor with her snake, Tremont. He was black, about seven feet long, and very much alive. People near her edged back a little in their chairs.

"It's Joyce!" said Pamela, in a loud whisper.

I looked at Tremont, and Tremont stared back at me with evil little eyes. "Joyce is a scaredy-cat?" I asked Pamela.

"She has always had a way with animals," said Pamela. "She loves animals."

Barnes nodded his approval. He'd be checking to see whether Tremont got proper rest, clean wholesome quarters, and the right kind of food to keep him healthy.

"Tremont is an animal?" I asked.

Pamela said, "Well, you know..."

While the snake coiled around her neck, slithered down and circled her waist, then worked its way back up to her shoulders, Francine-Joyce managed to unfasten one garment after another and drop it to the floor, swaying and rolling her hips as the music increased in tempo. She was soon down to the floor, where she eventually ended up on her back, her knees bent up and her legs apart. Tremont coiled and uncoiled be tween her legs, worked his way up until his little head was between her breasts, his tongue darting in and out with electronic rapidity. She began to churn her body in wild, orgiastic movements, straining her hips up against the snake as she moved faster and faster.

I glanced at Barnes. He was staring wide-eyed and unbelieving. I glanced at Pamela. She was studying the act with detached calm.

Francine-Joyce's climactic jerks finally ended, and the spots blacked out.

"I'll go back and talk to her first," said Pamela, pushing her chair back. "I can do more with her alone."

Barnes's eyes gradually came unglazed. I had a hunch duodenal spasms would follow, and offered him a Donnatal tablet. He accepted it, chewing it up in silence.

"Of the two girls' occupations, I have a feeling that Pamela's is probably the more honest," he said, after some thought.

The headwaiter came back with his microphone and told a few more flabby jokes while we waited. It seemed like a very long time, probably because the routine was so dull.

Pamela finally returned with Joyce, who was now dressed in street clothes. We stood up while she nervously acknowledged introductions, then sat down, expectantly.

"Joyce knows nothing about the robbery, but she knows why Bob Cressett is hiding," said Pamela.

"It's a frame-up, an out-and-out frame-up,"

said Joyce. She had much of Pamela's beauty, but her face was harder. Her long hair was brilliantly black.

"How can we help you?" asked Barnes, sounding as though he really meant it. Which he did.

"Keep Joyce out of it. She had nothing to do with it," said Pamela.

"Neither did Bob," said Joyce.

"Tell us about it," said Barnes.

"It started with that Perez thing. Somebody trying to make it look like Bob was collaborating with her to cheat the company out of ten thousand dollars. Then, the night of the robbery, Bob came here to pick me up after the last show." She scrabbled in her purse to find a cigarette, her hands trembling. I lit it for her. "We got in his car. I was out of cigarettes and I knew he kept a couple of spare packs in the glove compartment. I opened it to get one. There was a package of money in there." She puffed on her cigarette, inhaling nervously. "Bob knew for sure then that he was being set up for something."

"What time did he pick you up?" asked Barnes.

"About three-fifteen." The robbery had occurred between one-thirty and two.

"How much money was left in the car?"

"About five thousand dollars. In hundreds and fifties."

Barnes consulted his cigarette notebook. No

78

luck, the ten were already accounted for, and it was too early in the morning to begin on the next day's quota.

He sighed. "What did you do next?"

"We didn't know *what* to do. We drove over to Queens to one of those tremendous end-of-the-subway parking lots. We left the car there and took the subway back to my place. In the morning we heard about the robbery on the TV news. Then Bob *knew* he was being set up, and for something a lot worse than helping Mrs. Perez embezzle ten thousand dollars."

"Where is the money?"

"It's hidden."

"Where is Bob?"

Joyce stared at him, biting her lower lip. "If I tell you, how do I know—"

"Joyce, all I can promise you is that if he is innocent I'll do everything in my power to help him."

"What about Joyce? Will you keep her out of it?" asked Pamela.

Barnes switched his attention to Pamela. "If she's telling the truth, I think we can keep her out of it." He turned back to Joyce. "The money isn't hidden in your apartment, is it?"

Joyce blushed. I wouldn't have thought any girl who could carry on with a snake that way in public could blush, but she did.

"I see it is," said Barnes. "Well, you'd better let Pamela scoot over there and get it and bring it to us. We can't keep you from being involved if the money is hidden there, even if it is frame-up money."

Pamela nodded. "He's absolutely right, Joyce."

"In the meantime, it is essential that I talk to Cressett immediately."

"Are you going to turn him over to the police?"

"Not if I decide he's telling the truth."

"He *is* telling the truth. Why do you have to talk to him?"

Barnes was becoming impatient. "Because he may know something that will help me ferret out the man who is trying to set him up."

"I don't know—" said Joyce doubtfully.

"Listen," said Barnes, "I've promised to try to keep you out of it, and I've promised to try to help Bob Cressett. No more can I do. Without your cooperation I'll simply have to call Lieutenant Shunk and let him carry on from here."

"But you promised—" said Pamela.

"I promised to try to help you. If you won't cooperate, then I can't help you. And I'm certainly not going to jeopardize my license as a private investigator to help people who won't cooperate."

"You'd better tell him," said Pamela.

"He's holed up in a crummy room in the Village," said Joyce, "Christopher Street." I made a note of the number.

Joyce's apartment was on one of the Village side streets just off Fifth Avenue. We waited in the cab while Pamela went up to fetch the five thousand dollars. She returned in about ten minutes with a thick envelope held shut with a rubber band. We gave her the cab and sent her home, setting out for Christopher Street on foot.

"We'd make great mugging victims," I said, "with all that dough on hand."

Barnes smiled. "How's your karate?"

"Rusty. I haven't split any two-inch-thick planks recently."

"Then we'll just have to be alert."

It was a shabby old-law tenement, the kind the landlord has given up on and gone into hiding. Room 4-L was predictably on the fourth floor.

I knocked gently. There was no answer. I knocked again, louder. There was still no answer, and no sound of movement inside.

"Bob," I said, "Joyce sent us. It's urgent that we talk to you."

No sound. I strained to hear. Was he standing on the other side listening, possibly with a gun in his hand ready to blast right through the wood?

I knocked again, harder. Was it breathing I heard on the other side? I decided it was Barnes, who was probably sighing because he had run out of his quota of cigarettes. I turned the knob very slowly and quietly and pushed. The door was unlocked. I gave it a hard shove and stepped to one side, just in case.

Barnes, who was standing on the other side of the door, said, "Nobody home."

I looked in cautiously. The shabby one-room apartment was lighted by a single bulb hanging desolately in the center of the room. It seemed to be empty. Near the door there was a stained sink with a two-burner gas grill next to it. A dripping faucet was giving off a faint plopping sound. Under the sink a big fat roach hurried toward us. I moved to let him pass. The threadbare carpet was littered with newspapers and paperback books. Several saucers were overflowing with cigarette butts.

"Cressett has really been holing up," I said. "Joyce has probably been bringing him food. What a dump!"

We walked around, looking. There was no bathroom, and there were no closets. A large wardrobe stood in one corner, but aside from a single suit jacket, it was empty. A let-down bed stood upright at one end of the room, concealed by an arrangement of monk's-cloth drapes.

"Wonder if she changed her mind and managed to get word to him somehow?" asked Barnes.

"I doubt it."

"If he had the money, it certainly isn't here. Unless it's hidden in the bed somehow," said Barnes. "We'd better look."

I pulled aside the monk's cloth drapes and, grasping the folded legs at the top, lowered the bed.

As I bent over to settle them I heard Barnes say softly, "Oh my God."

Cressett was huddled on the bed near the head, where gravity had pulled him. His eyes were wide open and staring, and he was obviously dead. Blood and crushed bone on the left temple. A bedbug scurried out from beneath his neck and disappeared over the edge of the mattress.

Barnes stepped closer and stood studying the body.

"He put up quite a fight," he said after a moment.

One doubled-up fist was bloody and bruised. His upper lip bore the laceration of a blow. One shirt sleeve was ripped from shoulder to elbow. Buttons had popped from the shirt, exposing his stomach, where there was a dark, purple bruise the size of a baseball.

Barnes sighed deeply. "Well, there's nothing to do but call Shunk." He walked over to the wardrobe and, taking the envelope of money from his jacket, slipped it into the inside pocket of Cressett's jacket.

"Would you like to go call while I watch, or vice versa?" Barnes asked. "I don't care particularly about doing either."

"If I have a choice, you call, I'll watch." As

messy as the scene was, it was better than talking to Shunk. He was going to be one highly irritated cop.

Barnes was gone about ten minutes. I stood, shifting my feet from time to time to let the roaches go by. To sit down anywhere would mean maybe bringing home some bedbugs, which I can do without.

When he returned, Barnes was looking more cheerful. "I think we are in for a tongue-lashing," he said. "I told him the source of our information about Cressett's whereabouts was confidential. But that, of course, won't hold up."

"He has probably sent someone to pick up Pamela already."

"Of course."

"I hope they both have sense enough to keep quiet about the money."

"I do too," said Barnes. "I think Joyce was telling the truth about the extent of her involvement."

Shunk arrived with his whole crew before we could even brace ourselves. Tight-lipped, he ordered us to wait outside. The implication was that he would be out with his razor strop in due time.

We stood in the hall for a while, but the traffic in and out was so heavy we moved down to the street and paced in front of the building.

"This is a bore," said Barnes finally. He approached one of the cops sitting in a patrol car in

84

front of the building. "Tell Shunk we'll wait for him at headquarters."

"Just a minute, Mr. Barnes, I'll have to check." He spoke softly into a walkie-talkie, which must have had a mate up on the fourth floor, then listened as a slurred reply squawked inside the car.

"Lieutenant Shunk says we can drive you there. He doesn't want to lose contact."

We climbed in the back, and after motioning for another patrol car behind him to pull up in front of the building, the driver edged out into the early predawn emptiness of the street and took off at a good clip.

Sitting on the hard benches at headquarters was even more boring. Barnes, at least, was able to let his chin settle on his chest and take a short nap.

Shunk and two cops escorting Pamela arrived almost simultaneously.

She pointed at me and yelled, "That's the man! He assaulted me and ruptured my water bed!"

I stood up. "Pamela, how could you?"

"Not only that, he stole my checkbook and forged my name to a check for over three hun- dred and sixty dollars!"

"Pamela!"

"Search him! See if he hasn't got my check."

Shunk was enjoying the embarrassment so much he almost smiled. "You got her check, sonny?"

85

"Yes, but it isn't forged."

"If it ain't forged, what is it?"

"It's signed by her, and it isn't even made out to me. It's made out to *Knowledge Unlimited*. I sold her an encyclopedia set."

"You sold this chick an *encyclopedia*?"

"Yes, I did," I said, dripping as much sarcasm as would be healthy. "Avon Lady, huh?"

"He tried to rape me in six different closets. Then he ruptured my water bed," shouted Pamela.

Shunk stared at me, a faint but mean grin crinkling the corners of his mouth. "Lost control, eh, sonny?" He turned to Pamela. "You want to prefer charges, miss, and I'll throw his ass right in a cell."

"Now just a minute!"

"Of course I want to prefer charges." She turned to me. "You lying, untrustworthy psycho, you rapist type!"

Shunk was still grinning. I think he would have actually booked me, just for the hell of it. "Now look," I said to Pamela. "You have me arrested and I'm going to sue you for one million dollars. You'll have to work two or three years to make that much, and in the meantime you'll have to sell that IBM and everything, because when I sue, my lawyer will tie up all your assets."

She stood staring at me, her eyes getting narrower and narrower.

Barnes, who had been listening with a sleepy but amused smile on his face, stood up. "I think I can offer certain testimony which will tend to clear Larry."

In her rage, she hadn't noticed Barnes. She swung around and glared at him. "You're a skunk and a liar and a psycho! Just like your *assistant!*"

Barnes eyed her solemnly. "Miss Richards," he said, "we tried to protect our source of information, as we agreed. Unfortunately, we found Bob Cressett murdered. Bringing you in was Lieutenant Shunk's own idea."

"Bob murdered?" She looked hurriedly around at our faces. "Murdered?" She stumbled over to the bench and sank down, looking pale and exhausted. "Is Joyce—is Joyce all right?"

"Joyce!" yelled Shunk. He turned to Barnes. "So you *did* locate the sister. Now goddammit, where in the hell is she?"

Pamela told him.

Later, in his office, Shunk read us the Articles of War. We would be shot at sunrise, and Barnes wouldn't even be given a last cigarette to write in his goddamned notebook. He also read us sections of the code concerning revocation of licenses of private investigators.

Barnes argued that we couldn't have located Cressett so quickly otherwise, and that as soon as we pinned down his location we had planned to call Shunk. We had done it all for Shunk, Barnes explained, to help him find Cressett in a hurry. He was being basely ungrateful.

In a few minutes Shunk's steam subsided, and he began to expound his theories about the case. Cressett had done the dirty work, but he had been tied in with the Syndicate, or maybe even some ordinary crooks, who had helped him. Then they had knocked him off, and had taken all the money but five thousand dollars.

Barnes told him the story of the frame-up, without mentioning that Joyce had held the money for a time.

"And my hunch says she's telling the truth," he said.

Shunk thought about it. "Maybe she is. But maybe that's just what Cressett told *her*."

Barnes shook his head. "He was hardly the devious type who would have hidden five thousand dollars in the glove compartment for her to find, just to back up the story."

The morning sun was peeping timidly in the window. I yawned dramatically.

Shunk said, "Well, another night shot to hell."

On our way out, we passed Pamela and Joyce huddled together on the bench in the first floor hall. Pamela jumped up and hurried over to intercept us.

"I owe you an apology," she said.

"That's okay."

She asked Barnes in a whisper, "What happened to the money? Does he know Joyce had it?"

Barnes shook his head. "I left it in the room with Cressett."

She threw her arms around him and kissed him passionately.

While this was happening, he was giving me a nervous glance out of the corner of his eye. As we left the building I said, "I hope you didn't commit us for a thousand dollars. Ryan would never—"

By moving agilely I dodged a friendly boot in the rear.

4

Barnes graciously allowed us three hours of sleep. Just enough to make you feel completely rotten. At least, the shower and fresh clothes helped.

I met him as scheduled at nine-thirty in the lobby of the Consolidated building.

"Mr. Ryan isn't in," said the receptionist. "He went home ill."

Barnes hesitated. "I'd like to see Mr. Gates, then."

While she was ringing Gates's secretary, Tip Horgan came in. The area around his left eye was discolored with a purple-black glow, and one cheek sported a wide Band-aid. There was an unbandaged abrasion just above his red chin whiskers. I nudged Barnes.

He turned to look at Horgan.

"On second thought," he said to the receptionist, "tell Mr. Gates I'd like to see him later. Say in a half hour."

He stopped Tip, who was about to hurry past. "I think we should have a talk."

Tip paused, annoyed. "Later. I'm late, and I'm

way behind schedule. This damned robbery has screwed us up royally."

Barnes stared at him. "Immediately would be better."

Tip thought about it for a few seconds. "Oh hell," he said. "All right, but we'll have to make it fast."

We followed him upstairs to his small office. Barnes shut the door before we sat down.

"Why are you closing the door?" asked Tip.

Barnes smiled. "I'll open it if you wish. But since the matter is rather confidential—"

Tip shrugged.

"It would appear that you have been in a fight, or an accident."

Horgan's lower lip jutted slightly. "It would so appear," he agreed with a touch of sarcasm.

"Who were you fighting?"

"That is none of your damned business."

"Bob Cressett was killed last night."

"I know."

"There are indications that he had quite a fight with a man who killed him."

Horgan raised his red eyebrows, then touched the scraped area of his chin gingerly. "You think *I* killed Cressett?"

"I didn't say that. I asked for an explanation of your wounds."

Tip rubbed his forehead wearily. "Jesus, I've got a hangover to end all hangovers. It's none of your damned business, but I collected these wounds in a bar." He sighed deeply. "From a guy who didn't like the cut of my jib. Believe it or not, that's what he said."

"Where?"

"In the Village."

"What bar and what time?"

"I don't remember."

"Shunk can probably help you find it."

Tip glared at him. "You *are* being nasty."

Barnes consulted his cigarette notebook and entered the first smoke of the day. "Be reasonable. You've admitted to being in the Village, which puts you in the immediate area of the murder."

"Nevertheless," said Tip, "I do not care to elaborate on this theme."

Barnes lit his cigarette and stared at Tip thoughtfully. "You were in a bar, and you refuse to give the name of it."

"I told you, I don't remember."

"What street was it on?"

"I don't remember that either."

"Most convenient."

Tip flushed. "Listen, I've had just about enough of this. Cressett was found with money stolen from Consolidated in his possession. He was obviously tied in with the crooks who planned the robbery. They probably killed him because they couldn't trust him to keep his mouth shut."

"Indeed."

"Indeed, yes."

"I have certain doubts."

Tip stood up. "I must ask you to excuse me. As I told you, I'm way behind schedule."

We left, and went to see Gates.

His cheeks were not so pink this morning. He looked drawn and weary, and was still suffering from the head cold he had the night of the robbery. I had a couple of cold capsules at the ready, because Barnes would undoubtedly start sniffling as soon as we left him.

"This has been one bastard of a week," he said.

"It has," said Barnes. "What's wrong with Ryan?"

"He fell down the steps."

"What!"

"He was carrying that big manual collator down from the third floor. It's not heavy, but it's so big you can't see where you are going." Gates's mouth curled down at the corners. "He says he was pushed."

"Was he hurt?"

"Not badly. Broken front tooth, maybe a few sprains. He was limping a bit, but said he didn't think any bones were broken."

"Where were you when it happened?"

"In my office. I heard this crash, bang, thump, thump, and more crashing. I went out to see what was going on. He was lying at the bottom of the steps with the collator on top of him. I helped him up. He limped off to the bathroom to wash the blood off his face, cool as a cucumber."

"You don't think he was pushed?"

Gates blinked a few times. "Why would anyone push him? I think he simply made a misstep. It's easy to do that when you can't see where you're stepping."

"Hmmmm."

"You know how Ryan is. He never made a mistake in his life." Gates paused to blow his nose vigorously. "Where will it all end? We're in one hell of a mess. I'm half sick, and I don't know when we'll get caught up. We've probably got eight stores embezzling from us right now, and we're so far behind we won't know about it for a week."

Barnes made sympathetic sounds.

"Not only that, sales are down."

"Dave, for the record I'm going to have to ask you where you were last night."

Gates blinked again, surprised. "Me? At home."

"Anyone with you?"

"My wife. The kids are grown up and married."

"I've often wondered, just where do you live, Dave?"

"Brooklyn Heights." He smiled. "You surely don't think I killed Bob Cressett? I'm so old and decrepit I can hardly get myself on the subway to go home nights."

Barnes smiled. "You look pretty fit to me."

"I couldn't punch my way out of a paper bag."

Barnes stood up. "When do you think Ryan will be back?"

Gates glanced away. "Tomorrow, I hope. Said he just wanted to have his doctor check him over."

We made our way to the office we had set up in Ryan's conference room. Tony Wilson, Harry Weiner, and Bill Perkes were there, waiting for instructions. A faint aroma of alcohol surrounded Tony, but he seemed sober enough. Harry Weiner was dark, with razor-scraped blue-black jowls, and Bill Perkes had an Adam's apple which bobbed when he talked.

"I have a line on Cressett's girl friend," said Perkes. "She's a nightclub entertainer. Works in a joint called the Naked Owl."

Barnes sighed deeply. They needed a lot of bringing up to date. After he spent five minutes doing just that, he picked up their written reports and studied them.

I sat waiting, my eyelids getting pretty heavy. Three hours isn't proper sleep for a growing boy.

"The theory," said Barnes, "is that Cressett was acting as inside man for some underworld types who engineered this thing." He tapped the papers in front of him. "I don't see any off-beat connections in any of these friends or relatives."

"Absolutely none," said Harry Weiner.

"Other than Joyce Richards, of course," said Barnes.

"Yeah," said Perkes, "A lot of these crummy dives are owned by the Mafia."

Barnes thought some more, then sent them off to mine the same ground more thoroughly. Perkes was to check the ownership of the Naked Owl carefully, from possible dummy owner up to the real cash behind it. Weiner was to check Cressett's friends in more depth, their relatives and connections. Harry Wilson he advised to drink a pot of black coffee, then concentrate on Cressett's neighborhood contacts; the dry cleaner, laundry, apartment house super, anyone who had any dealings with him.

After they left I said, "I thought you were satisfied that Cressett was framed?"

"True," he said, "but as Shunk would say, we must leave no stone unturned. Anyway, if Cressett was set up, it's just possible that investigating his contacts may lead us to whoever tried it."

"Madam Perez would be an important link."

"Right. But she's a tough old bat. She has her ten thousand and I suspect that nothing short of the Chinese water torture would get anything out of her."

I shook my head. "She might panic. This has grown from a ten-thousand-dollar diddle to possible prosecution as an accessory in two murders."

Barnes sneezed a couple of times. All the time his subconscious had been hard at work on his exposure to Gates's cold. I handed him two placebos. "Here, you'd better take some more cold pills," I said.

He accepted them and chewed them up absentmindedly.

"It's possible. We can try leaning on her a bit."

I was still sleepy, and not exactly cerebrating with full power. "If it's a frame-up, it seems to me that the field is pretty well narrowed down to Tip Horgan or Gates. Or Ryan," I added laughing. "And Gates, being a weak old man—"

"Gates is not a weak old man. Don't let his white hair and pink cheeks mislead you. He's only fifty-one."

"Oh."

"I've seen him toss sixty-pound bags of silver around the way a supermarket clerk might handle a pound of sugar."

I used the necessary eye muscles to keep my eyelids propped open.

"Keep in mind that there are other options open. Duplicate keys, help from the inside by some other employee."

"What about the time lock?"

"Jamming of the time lock happened periodically. Suppose, for instance, that the robbery was planned on a contingency basis. For the next time the lock acted up? A quick telephone call from any one of a number of employees there at closing time could set it up."

"They only had four weeks to get duplicates to fit the new locks."

"Long enough."

The thought of having maybe ten or fifteen suspects instead of two made me even more weary. "My bets are on Horgan or Gates."

He smiled. "We've certainly got to do some checking on Tip's alleged bar brawl."

One lead to Horgan's off-duty life was his interest in acting. He had mentioned modestly that he was a fine actor the night we called on Serena Perez. In checking backgrounds Barnes had discovered that Horgan was believed to have had roles in several off-off Broadway productions. But that's as far as the information went.

"Suppose you trot down to the Village and make the rounds of off-off Broadway theaters. See if you can locate some fellow thespians who know Tipton, what he's up to and where he's at. When he's not being a Consolidated supervisor and arrogant heir to untold millions."

"Thespians?"

"Actors."

I knew that, of course. It just bugs me when Barnes talks that way. Also, I never trot.

I started with La Mama and visited about six two-by-four theaters before lunch. Actually I went to ten, but four were locked up with nobody home. Basement rooms, attic rooms, storefront auditoriums with folding chairs, church parish rooms, and even one located in a former undertaking establishment. It was called the Liberated Coffin, and some kind of nude show was in rehearsal. I spent quite a bit of time there questioning all the girls, but none of them had heard of Tipton Horgan.

Two hamburgers and two cups of coffee later I wandered into a theater which had been converted from a small cheese warehouse, and still offered some faint aromas from the rich old Italian cheeses which had been stored there. It was called the Gay-Itty.

They were rehearsing a powerful homosexual play about a man who ends up castrating his lover. At the point where I came in they were having quite an argument about the castration scene, whether it should be handled with bloody violence, or in quiet good taste to drive home the deep poignancy and tragedy.

One of the actors noticed me and strolled over.

"How do you think it should be handled?" he asked. He was tall, muscular, blond, and handsome enough to stop any girl, but not for long.

"I'd vote for quiet good taste. Not only will it be more poignant, but the technical problems involved in the other. Cleaning up all that ketchup after every performance." I shook my head.

He laughed. "I agree." He looked me over carefully. "What can we do for you?"

I held out my hand. "I'm Larry Howe. I'm prowling around looking for an old friend. I hear he's been acting in off-Broadway productions."

We shook hands. "I'm Marcel Proust. That's my legal name. I changed it to avoid problems."

"Problems?"

"Mainly the problem of embarrassing my parents. I've come out."

"Liberating the gay?"

"I see you're not with it."

"No. But I'm not a homophobe."

He smiled. "But you wouldn't want your brother to marry one?"

That stumped me. "I'd take a strong stand with regard to my sister," I said.

He grinned. "So would I." He blinked for a second or two and then said, "Well, who are you looking for?"

"A fellow named Tipton Horgan."

There was a noticeable frosting over.

"Don't think I know him."

I turned to the group who were still arguing and yelled, "Any of you guys know Tip Horgan?"

They stopped arguing. One of them called, "What did you say about Tip Horgan?"

"I'm looking for him."

Marcel Proust was embarrassed. "Space it," he called loudly, "This dude's not one of us."

He took my arm and turned me toward the door. "Nobody here knows Tip Horgan. And this is a private rehearsal on private property. Au revoir."

"When you see Tip, tell him I've been looking for him."

He walked me to the door, still holding my arm, his smile a bit grim.

So Tipton was one of them, but not ready to go public. I wondered if old General Ellsworth knew? It could be a great setup for blackmail, if he didn't. Along in years, the General could easily be the type who would look upon this as moral degeneracy of the lowest order. Reason not only for disinheritance, but for complete disassociation. I do not *have* a grandson, sir! It could be that Tip might need a half million dollars in a hurry. Ransom for his secret could come high.

What next? I decided I had better report back to Barnes.

On the subway I changed my mind and stayed on past Thirty-fourth Street. Why not go up to Harlem and see Serena? Confront her with my knowledge. Tipton Horgan was the man who let her sign the promissory note, and has thus involved her in a double murder. She'd confess all. Assistant solves case. That would show Shunk the Skunk.

102

What about Ed and his homicidal fists? That morning I had for no particular reason clipped on my .38 shoulder holster, for which I am duly licensed. A touch of clairvoyance. If big Ed got frisky, I'd wave the firearm around.

Serena Perez's store was even dustier than before. And empty. The bell in the back activated by the door rang briefly when I entered, but no one appeared. After waiting five minutes, I went back to the door and opened it, holding it so that the bell would continue to ring. After another minute or two, one of the biggest blacks I have ever seen came sauntering out to the counter. He was side-shouldered, with an Afro haircut which must have added about four inches to his six-one or -two height.

"Man, you irritating me holding that bell," he said.

I shut the door. I didn't want to irritate him.

"I want to see Serena Perez."

"Not here."

"When will she be back?"

"Not coming back."

"What do you mean, not coming back?"

He screwed up his Swiss chocolate face. "Man, don't you speak English? I say she gone, she not coming back. You want me to tell about it in French?" He told me about it in French.

"Oh," I said.

"Now I tell it to you in German. Hear this, *Dumbkopf, Frau Perez nicht hier. Verstehen?*"

His French was too fast for me, and my German is pretty rusty, but I got the Dumbkopf part all right. Afro snobs are the worst kind.

"Now just a minute. She owns this store."

"No she don't."

"Who does?"

"I do."

I glanced around at the sparse inventory. "She can't sell this store. We've got a lien on it that would make the Tower of Pisa feel insecure. This store owes Consolidated ten thousand bucks."

He grinned, spreading a row of big white teeth all over his face. "Oh, you the man from Consolidated. I heard about that little contretemps."

"You'll be hearing more about it, as time goes on."

He came out from behind the counter quickly and walked past me to the door. Before I realized what he was up to he thrust a key into it and shot the double-locking bolts home. Then he pocketed the key in his tight jeans and turned to me.

"I think you want to come and have a talk with the boss."

I wasn't sure I wanted to. "Unlock that door," I said. "I don't like your attitude. I mean, I don't like being locked in."

"You got claustrophobia?"

"Open that door."

He studied me, still grinning. "Man, I got to lock the door when I take you to the boss. We go out the back door and upstairs. I leave this door unlocked, somebody come in and steal what little we got left."

That was better. All the time I thought he was locking the door so nobody could come in when I started yelling for help.

Another black, not so tall but also with an Afro hair ball, came from the back room. He looked at me silently.

"Cyril, I want you to meet Harvey Motherbanger. From Consolidated Money Orders," said the first black.

"Welcome to our humble establishment, Harvey Motherbanger," said the second.

"Thanks," I said. "Unlock the door."

"I think we take Harvey up to see Spinoza."

"I just remembered I have another appointment. Unlock the door."

Cyril moved out from behind the counter. "Well, let's get it on, man."

They surrounded me. Giant on my right, Cyril on my left, both clutching an arm.

I wear it so seldom, I had completely forgotten my compact little Smith & Wesson. The thought soothed some of the panic which had been settling in.

"This way, Harvey," said Cyril, pushing me toward the curtained doorway behind the counter.

The back room had a few pieces of wicker furniture and some cartons of canned goods. At the rear a narrow hall led to a bedroom, which seemed to be musty and unused. The bed was stripped to the mattress, and the two wooden chairs were coated with dust. Opposite the entrance to this room was a door. Cyril manipulated two keys in a heavy double lock and opened it. We were now in the back hall of a building facing on the next street. With Cyril leading the way, we climbed to the fourth floor, then went down the hall to the front of the building. At 4-A he pressed the buzzer in a long and complicated signal that had too many dots and dashes for anyone to remember, or even recognize. Probably the Gettysburg Address.

The small black man who opened it stared at me and then gave a whoop of recognition.

"Spinoza *McWilliams!*" I yelled.

He held his hands out, palms up. I slapped them and we danced around a little, the way blacks do.

Spinoza McWilliams was about five feet four, and skinny. He was dressed immaculately in a fawn-colored suit, tattersall vest, yellow shirt with a dark red tie. His hair, which was by no means Afro, had a configuration uniquely his own. It stood up on both sides in a V formation.

"Spinoza, you been writing checks again," I said, looking him over.

He howled and slapped his knee. When Spinoza was thirteen he almost matriculated in the wrong kind of school. He was writing rubber checks for very small amounts and cashing them in candy stores all over Harlem. He even gave one to the local numbers runner, and that was the last bad check he ever wrote, or so the story went.

He straightened up. "Abdul, you and Cyril go back to the store. I know this cat from way back."

The two men, who had been watching our reunion with amused smiles, turned to go. "Harvey, we see you later maybe," said Abdul.

I followed Spinoza through the small foyer to an office about thirty by twenty which would have satisfied a General Motors vice-president. Oak paneling, bookshelves set into the wall, a tremendous half-moon desk in gleaming walnut, thickly cushioned swivel chair with headrest, stereo, television, bar, leather sofas, marble coffee tables, and even a couple of issues of *Fortune*.

I stared around in amazement. "You're really far out."

He settled into the big swivel chair. "I do pretty good, man."

I glanced around, still taking it all in. On one wall there was a set of crossed foils. Anywhere else it would have been decoration. For Spinoza, it was appropriate. He had been captain of the fencing team at Cheshire College.

Being lazy, and having to take some kind of physical ed, I had opted for fencing. I had had the naive idea that it wouldn't be too strenuous.

You know, just stand there and wave a sword around for a while. After I got over my dismay at finding that it was more strenuous than a fast set of tennis, I got interested. In time I had learned a lot from Spinoza, even got to be second man on the team.

"Looks like you've made it big," I said, wondering how. Cressett had thought the store was a numbers drop. Was Spinoza some kind of executive in the Black Mafia?

He smiled. "Larry, you want a drink, you go over to the bar and help yourself."

"Maybe later."

"How long has it been? Four years?"

"At least."

"What you doing up here?"

"Trying to find Serena Perez. I'm a P.I. on a job for Consolidated Money Orders."

"You the man from Consolidated?" He laughed and slapped his knees some more. "No shit!"

"What's so funny?"

"You being a big detective."

I smiled.

"I like you better with your guitar."

"Yeah. Well, I decided to settle down and eat regularly." I glanced around. "What's with all the affluence? Last time I saw you, you were a poor boy working your way through college."

He waved one hand negligently. "Investments, man, investments."

We sat and talked about the good old days for a while. During the three years we had known each other we had gotten to be pretty good friends, everything considered. I mean the reservations a black has about whites, and vice versa, buried deep in the subconscious if not on the surface. On the surface we were good friends and I, at least, had no conscious reservations.

"Abdul says he bought the store from Serena Perez. She had no right to sell it," I said, getting back to the purpose of my visit.

"He just talking."

"He doesn't own it?"

He shook his head. "Serena took off. Nobody know where she's gone. I own some buildings around here, including the one her store is in. I figure no rent, I might as well put Abdul in there. That way I get my rent for a while."

I smiled. "Hey, wait a minute. Whatever inventory she's got there belongs to Consolidated."

"No shit?"

"She owes us ten thousand dollars."

He laughed, delighted with the thought. "She owes me too. I got a prior claim."

"How come?"

"Possession is nine points of the law, man. I'm in possession."

I shrugged. I'm not the lawyer. Let Barnes worry about that angle. With over five hundred thousand dollars missing, the nine hundred or a thousand bucks they might get from Serena's inventory was a minor matter. Spinoza might be in on the whole deal; the embezzlement, the framing of Cressett. The whole half million might be stashed away right in this apartment.

Spinoza, who had an I.Q. of one hundred and sixty, had graduated in the top of his class. A philosophy major. At that time he had planned to stay on and work for a Ph.D. I wondered what shunted him back to Harlem. Blacks were getting much more encouragement and help toward academic jobs today than in the past. It was probably the usual frustrations of the black man. He had never been the faculty tea type, that was for sure. He like his joint, and no interference, man. He could speak like a cultured Englishman when he chose. He chose to stick to Harlemese.

Spinoza was far too shrewd to tell me anything he didn't want me to know. If we got anything out of what I had learned so far, it would be in establishing a connection between Tip Horgan and Spinoza.

"Which one of these monkeys got away with the half million?" he asked.

"What do you mean?"

"That Consolidated thing. It was an inside job, wasn't it?"

"Well—" I searched for an answer. "Why?"

"I got sort of a financial interest in Consolidated."

"How so?"

He giggled. "Maybe we want to put money orders back in that store."

I laughed. "Not a chance."

"Don't be so sure of that, man. I got influence."

"Ryan would have apoplexy."

He slid down a little in his huge chair. "That Ryan. He just a big shuck."

"You know Ryan? Personally?"

His eyes narrowed, but he was still grinning. "I've had some dealings with him."

"What kind of dealings?"

"Man, you're inquisitive. Fact is, I had to guarantee Serena's financial reliability. I'm sort of a cosigner, you might say."

"You mean, *you're* stuck for the ten thousand?"

"Shit, no! My lawyer got a few little clauses in that contract Ryan never noticed."

It was strange we hadn't heard this part of the arrangement. Still, Serena had been handling Consolidated money orders for two years. When Ryan reread the contract, perhaps he was too embarrassed to mention that she had a guarantor, he *thought*.

Spinoza fumbled in his vest pocket and brought out a small plastic envelope. From the other side of his vest he extracted a tiny gold spoon. Dipping it daintily in the envelope he removed it full of white powder. He then placed the packet carefully on the desk and raised his free hand to close his left nostril, brought the

111

spoon up tightly against the right, took a loud sniff, and sighed. Then he repeated the procedure, sniffing another spoonful into the left nostril.

As he folded the packet and stuffed it back in his vest pocket I said, "Sorry to see you on the hard stuff, Spinoza."

"You *sorry*."

"Yeah, I'm sorry."

"You white honkies drove me to it. Mind you, I ain't mainlining."

"You know damned well I'm no white honky."

"You white honky like all the rest."

"Come off it!"

"What I do is none of your business, white boy."

"You dealing in the stuff?"

He jumped up, his grin gone. "You just like all the rest. You see a black man who's made it big, you assume he made it in dope, procuring, or the numbers, or all three." He walked around his big desk and stood over me. "You go back and tell Ryan he want his ten thousand he come see me. That lousy ten thousand ain't nothing to me." He snapped his fingers under my nose. "Nothing, you hear? I make more than that in a week."

I stood up and edged past him. "Okay," I said. "I still hate to see you on the hard stuff."

He strolled over to the far wall, bouncy legged, and lifted down the foils. "You pretty good foilsman, I'll say that for you, whitey."

"Quit calling me whitey."

"We had some pretty good time, didn't we, boy?" He handed me one of the foils.

I looked it over curiously. The point was as sharp as an ice pick. "Yeah, we did. You made a good fencer out of me."

He moved about six feet away, and with a little leap, spread his legs in the fencing position "I'm gonna give you a chance to show what a good fencer I made out of you. *En Garde!*" He raised his foil in the customary salute.

He had to be kidding.

"I said *en garde,* you white shit."

"You out of your mind? No buttons, no mask? You want somebody to get killed, or lose an eye?" That was pretty strong stuff he had been sniffing.

"Defend yourself, whitey. Bring that foil up before I put mine right through your liver." He made a fast feint, then began his attack with a quick jump lunge. I parried. What the hell else could I do?

"Cut it out, Spinoza! Be reasonable!"

"Pretty soon you be hollering for your mama. I'm gonna cut you, man!" He began a steady marching attack with straight thrusts, disengages, cutovers. Rusty, it was all I could do to parry, much less riposte. Sweat began to pop out

113

on my forehead as I beat that needle point off course again and again. He marched, I retreated. He attacked, I parried.

We circled the office, with me moving backward, which is definitely a disadvantage. I hadn't fenced in more than two years. My legs ached and my right arm felt leaden, and sweat was running into the corners of my eyes and burning like hell, not to mention what it did to my vision.

I began to get mad. "You lousy bastard, you're cheating!" I yelled.

"What you mean, cheating?" He made another jump lunge.

I parried. "You're high on smack. I'm fighting under my own steam."

He began another running attack, while I retreated, parrying like crazy. Must have been about my fiftieth backward circle of the room. "I take that steam out of you," he yelled. "You gonna be colder than a frozen codfish when I finish."

Exhaustion was beginning to slow my reflexes. The needle point ripped through my left sleeve. I tried attacking, but he was too fast for me. The needle point nicked my earlobe. Retreat some more, with blood running down my jaw and neck.

"I fix the other ear now," said Spinoza, gasping. "We bury you with earrings on so you look pretty."

I tried closing in, where my weight and height

would give me an advantage. At least it gave me a few seconds of rest while we grunted, eyeball to eyeball, foil guards locked and straining.

"Who cheating now?"

Closing in calls for a penalty in a legitimate fencing match. This one was highly illegitimate to begin with. I reached out with my left hand and grabbed his skinny throat. Another thing a decent sort of foilsman wouldn't do.

"Auwwwk," he grunted as I squeezed his tonsils hard. Now *he* was backing away. With a quick twist he managed to jerk away and free his foil.

He coughed a couple of times, then began another attack. I closed in again, and while we were straining I kicked him hard in the shin.

He jerked away, doing a fast, limping back-up. "Man, you fight dirty."

"You're goddamned right!" I yelled. I decided the next time I was able to close in I would give him a belt in his most vulnerable area, a place guaranteed to give him an excruciating stomach-ache.

He started a whirlwind running attack, and it was all I could do to keep that ice-pick from going into an eye and right through my brain. I deflected it left, deflected it right, deflected it upward, where it put another part in my hair. This man was bent on homicide, there was no escaping it.

When he slowed a fraction I closed in again,

115

my right arm straining to keep the foil guards locked. Swinging my left fist low, I belted him as hard as I could in the crotch.

He let out a high-pitched scream and doubled over. I dropped my foil and did some fancy backward running, clutching at my holster frantically. I had the .38 out just before I tripped over one of his coffee tables. Luckily I was able to hold on to it, and broke the fall with my outstretched left hand. I rolled quickly, and had the .38 pointed at him in a fraction of a second.

He was sitting on the floor keening and holding his stomach.

I got to my knees cautiously, then to my feet, still pointing that great little Smith & Wesson at him.

"Man, you just about castrated me," he groaned.

I was still puffing. "You need to see your shrink. I mean, they ought to lock you away somewhere."

Still clutching his stomach, he gasped. "From this day on, you, man, are marked for extinction. You have become extinct, even to the fifth generation."

I edged backward to the door, keeping the revolver pointed at him.

"Extinct. Even to the fifth generation if you manage to plant your seed before I get you," he said in a singsong moan.

5

Down in the rattling clamor of the subway I felt depressed, bruised, and sick. Old Spinoza. Not only on heroin, but out to kill me, for no reason at all. My leg and arm muscles ached painfully, and my collar was still damp with blood.

Stepping into a steaming shower, I was still numbly fascinated with the situation. During the hundreds of times I had fenced with Spinoza and others, I had often wondered how it would feel if the duel was for real. No buttons, no mask, and to the death. Like in the old days. Now I knew.

It was unsporting of me to cop out. But it was a setup for Spinoza. He had obviously kept in practice. And he had been better than me even when I was at my best. The lousy little bastard was out to kill me. And what had I ever done to him?

I toweled myself dry, put some witch hazel on my ear, which had stopped bleeding, put my shirt in some cold water to soak the blood out, and dressed.

It was only four o'clock. Time to report back to Barnes, as though I hadn't already put in a week's work in one afternoon. I mean, how often should a private investigator have to fight a duel to the death with unbuttoned foils? I was tired. It might be that I was in the wrong kind of occupation. I mean, a little violence and danger now and then is fine, but this case was providing too much of a good thing. Wicher's head smashed in, Cressett's head smashed in, me almost skewered like a damned shish kebab by a crazy black; enough is enough.

I found Barnes and Shunk in Ryan's conference room. Barnes was making a lot of notes and going at the situation very scientifically, which he rarely does unless he's completely stumped.

I listened for a few minutes while Barnes worried out loud and chewed the end of his ballpoint pen. When he is in one of his "let's get it all down on paper and analyze it" moods, he only half listens to me. I wanted his full attention for my big news about Tip Horgan and Madam Perez.

"According to the records of the answering service, Ryan called the Denzer people at nine o'clock, again at ten-thirty, and again at twelve. They didn't get there until after two," said Barnes. "Were they legitimately that busy? Five hours to answer a call?"

Shunk scratched his chin. "They could have made it earlier. There was some sort of mixup. Ryan left word that they were to call him before coming. They claim they tried to call a couple of times and couldn't reach him."

"Why did Ryan do that?"

"He wanted to explain the nature of the problem. He says they're like plumbers. They come, look the job over, then have to go back for more tools or parts."

"Hmmmm." He studied his notes some more. "This Doris Preeble. I think I'll have a talk with her."

"Who is Doris Preeble?" I asked.

Shunk grunted.

"She's a witness who didn't see anything," said Barnes. He explained that in the questioning of all the inhabitants of the block, particularly those with windows fronting on the street, Doris Preeble was the only one who admitted to being awake between 1 and 2 A.M. Her apartment was on the second floor front, almost directly across the street from Consolidated.

"Wasting your time," said Shunk. "The fact that she didn't see anything is meaningless. Obviously she wouldn't be watching the street the whole time."

"Hmmmm," said Barnes. He shuffled his notes some more and sighed deeply. Then he turned to me. "Well, what did you discover about Tip, if anything?"

If anything. Did he have a surprise coming. With modest down-playing of the incidents, I told them about Tip, about my visit to the Perez store, my duel to the death with Spinoza McWilliams.

While I was describing our duel, Shunk began to laugh.

"It wasn't all that funny," I said. "Spinoza is one of the best foilsman in the country. You wouldn't think it was so funny if he was trying to put a rapier through *your* liver."

Shunk barked some more. After a moment he recovered from his delight at the idea of my being skewered mortally by a mad black and said, "So Tipton is a closet queen. This bears looking into."

Barnes nodded. "It would seem that Madam Perez and Spinoza McWilliams bear even more looking into."

"Oh, we'll find her."

"I think you might even pick up Spinoza McWilliams. Assault with intent to kill," said Barnes.

I showed them the jagged little cut on my ear. "Three inches or so to the left and I would have swallowed a sword."

Shunk barked again. "We could," he said, containing himself. "Of course he'd be out on bail in ten minutes. We might get more by leaving him loose for the time being."

"There's Larry's safety to consider. McWilliams has threatened to kill him," said Barnes.

120

"Not only me, but five generations of me."

"Probably an idle threat," said Shunk.

Considering all the jumping around we did, I thought that was a singularly inappropriate adjective. "Not idle," I said, "it was a hard-working threat."

Shunk said, "Well, of course, if Larry wants to prefer charges—"

"Forget it. As you say, he'd be out in ten minutes."

"We'll certainly keep an eye on him."

Barnes stood up. "One thing we should check immediately. Whether Tip actually had a fight in a bar. He could have been reluctant to name the place, if it's a known homo hangout." He turned to Shunk. "Otto, if you'd give Larry a list of such places, he can start checking."

Barnes was getting to be a real pain in the rear. Couldn't he see I was exhausted? I wearily wrote down the names Shunk reeled off, about ten places.

"Those are the only ones I can think of at the moment. I'll have the boys prepare a complete list, but you can start with them," he said.

Barnes, who is quite sensitive to nuances of feeling, spotted my barely concealed hostility. "What's the matter?"

"Fighting a duel is pretty exhausting. Then, of course, I've lost a certain amount of blood."

That brought the house down, with Shunk

yelping like a dog with his tail caught in the door, and Barnes grinning like a clown.

Barnes clapped me on my sore right shoulder. "Tell you what, we'll both go, and I'll buy you a smashing dinner."

We took a cab to the Village and started the rounds. Surprisingly, we made a good pair for the job. Barnes, a distinguished looking middle-aged man, me a sullen-faced young pickup. I didn't have to act, either, man. I was feeling sullen. Three hours' sleep the night before, and the hardest day I ever had in my life.

The first place was called Homme du Monde, and we drew a blank. Jesus, the Puerto Rican bartender, was friendly enough and honest, I believe, in never having heard of Tip Horgan.

Our next stop, the Sodomerry Bar, was also unproductive. While Barnes was getting friendly with the bartender, a guy tried to pick me up. "Dust off that square and come up to my place," he suggested. I told him that my friend was insanely jealous, and as vicious as a piranha when crossed in love. "The last time a guy tried to pick me up, my friend set fire to his cummerbund," I said. "The poor boy couldn't wear a belt for *weeks.*"

He moved hastily down the bar. When Barnes brushed against him coming back, he squeaked.

"What's the matter with him?" Barnes asked me.

"I don't know. Did you try to get familiar with him?"

We then went to a place called En Garçon, and had a really great dinner. I'd give them four stars in my guidebook. But if any of the waiters, the bartender, or the proprietor knew Tip Horgan, they were too discreet to reveal such knowledge. Anyway, the bottle of wine we had with dinner was excellent, and my spirits were considerably improved by the good food and drink. We trudged somewhat wearily on to the next stop, the Phallustrader. The bar was fairly empty, but there was our man. He was nursing a martini, and looked like a guy who had been riding a motorcycle west in the eastbound lanes of the thruway. He had a black eye, a very large swollen nose, his arm in a sling, and scrape marks from the concrete on his forehead.

Barnes pounced. "Say, you're the guy who went ten rounds with Tip Horgan last night!"

The victim put his martini down. "Did you see it?"

"No, I heard about it."

"I'm looking for witnesses."

"He says you started it."

The victim picked up his martini. "That's a goddamned lie if I ever heard a goddamned lie. I made an innocent remark, that's all. I'm going to sue the son of a bitch for every penny he's got!"

We ordered a couple of Scotches on the rocks.

"I can't get any witnesses. Nobody wants to get *involved.*"

Barnes consulted his cigarette notebook and found that he had some options left. He lit one with quiet satisfaction. "I can't imagine a gentle fellow like Tip starting a brawl. I know he's an excellent boxer, but—"

"He did, dammit, right out of the blue. I was just being campy and said, 'Tip, I don't like the cut of your jib.' Then, whammo, right in the face!"

Barnes took his name and address just in case, and assured him that if we ran across any witnesses, we'd let him know. Carpenter Meret, the name our loser gave, offered to cut us in on his damages if we found him a witness willing to testify.

"I hear Horgan is rich," he said, "I think he may have deviated my septum. If he's damaged my septum, he's got to pay."

We finished our drinks and left. I was wondering vaguely what a septum was, and when I got home I looked it up. A membrane that divides liquids, like an osmosis, or something. A strayed membrane. Oh well. I called Isabel to say good night, which was customary with us when I was working, and then went to sleep.

Ryan was fairly irritable when we saw him the next morning. He had a sizable gap in his upper front teeth, very puffy lips, blue bruises on one cheek, and a few small lacerations over the right temple.

"This thing doesn't seem to be progressing at all, Barnes," he said. "Nothing has happened since you located Cressett. I want to know who he was tied in with." His voice began to rise. "I want to know who's got our dough!"

Barnes stared at his damaged face. "Sorry to hear about your accident."

"It was no accident. I was pushed, dammit."

"Are you certain it wasn't just a misstep?"

"Certainly I'm certain. I was feeling around carefully for the next step down, and I felt a definite light shove in the back. It was just enough to make me miss the step."

"Did you see anyone nearby when you started down the steps?"

"No." He hesitated. "Well, that is, only Dave Gates. He came out of his office and said something just before I was pushed."

"Then if anyone pushed you, Dave would have seen them?"

"Not necessarily. Maybe he had turned to go back into his office."

"But he would have seen someone else in the hall."

Ryan thought about that. "I don't know. All I know is that I was pushed, dammit."

"Could Dave have pushed you?"

"Don't be ridiculous."

Barnes got out his cigarette notebook, glanced at his watch, and noted down the time carefully. Then he fished out a filter-tip and lit it.

"Rod, I don't believe Cressett was tied in with anyone. I think he was meant to be the fall guy for this whole operation."

Ryan's mouth curved downward impatiently. "Shunk told me your theory. I don't buy it. The guy had some of our dough in his possession. That's good enough for me."

Cressett's car had been in the Consolidated parking lot at the time of the robbery. Theoretically someone could have stashed a small packet of money in his glove compartment in a matter of a minute or two. But Barnes evidently decided there was no use arguing. "We're checking every source, every contact Cressett ever had," he said. He then told Ryan about my visit to the Perez store and Spinoza McWilliams. He said nothing about what we had learned of Tip Horgan's situation.

"I was surprised to hear that Mrs. Perez had a guarantor."

Ryan blushed. "That lousy little creep McWilliams. Some guarantor!"

"Shafted you?"

"He's a black-hearted, black-faced little bastard of a crook. Not worth the paper it's written on. If I had known then what I—" Ryan stopped suddenly and snapped his mouth shut.

"If you had known what?"

Ryan stood up. "I've got a business to run. I can't spend any more time with you right now. Find those goddamned crooks who got to Cressett. Find our dough!" He stomped angrily out of the conference room.

I gave Barnes two Gelusil tablets to chew up. When a client is unhappy with our progress, Barnes's stomach begins to act up. This might even be a Pepto-Bismol day, with Donnatal pills thrown in to quiet duodenal spasms.

"It would seem that Tip's injuries were legitimate," I said. "Maybe Ryan only pretended to fall down the stairs. He could have thrown the collator down the steps, then hurried down and assumed a prone position under it before Gates got there."

Barnes finished chewing up his Gelusil. "Gates said his face was bloody."

"I noticed a couple of foil packets of ketchup in his secretary's desk the other night."

Barnes smiled.

"Well, it's got to be Horgan, Gates, or Ryan," I said. "Who knows, maybe Ryan's in trouble financially."

"Could be."

Barnes spent the next ten minutes studying his notes and saying nothing. My eyelids drooped. I was still sleepy.

Horgan eased in and closed the door quietly.

That woke me up.

He pulled a chair out from under the table and sat down, facing Barnes, a shy half smile on his face.

"I—I'd like to have a little chat."

Barnes, who had been watching him, said, "Certainly."

Horgan fiddled with one of the buttons on his jacket for a few seconds, staring at it and down at the table. The button was loose, about to fall off, but I don't think he was really seeing it. "I don't know quite how to put this, but, well, I'd like to ask a favor of you."

Barnes smiled. "All right, go ahead."

"I understand Ryan has told you in confidence—" he hesitated —"that is, he has explained my position here."

Barnes shuffled his notes together and turned the pile face down. "He has. If you're referring to the fact that General Ellsworth is your grandfather."

Horgan clenched and unclenched his right fist, which was now resting on the table. "Yes. That's it. I'd like to request that you be very careful with this information. It's important to me that no one here knows. I'd very much
ap preciate it if you would not tell *anyone*."

Barnes nodded. "I certainly won't mention it if it has no bearing on the case."

"It has no bearing whatsoever."

"Then you can depend on us."

"I mean, I'd hate to be known around here as the big boss's grandson."

"I can understand that."

"All my life I have been plagued by being the grandson of a hundred-million-dollar fortune."

I wished he would blow some of that plague my way.

"You don't know how refreshing it has been, being incognito, so to speak. People like you or dislike you for your qualities as a human being, not because you have expectations of being very rich. I never realized what a difference it made until I started working here." He flashed a somewhat forced and slightly pained smile at Barnes. "Wish I'd learned the difference sooner."

Barnes studied him gravely. "Yes, I see."

He went on. "I remember a girl I was quite in love with when I was in college. She—well we were at a dance, and I overheard"—he paused, rubbing his chin thoughtfully—"I was on the terrace, taking in some fresh air. Jan, the girl I was with, and another girl were inside, standing right next to an open French door. The other girl made some disparaging remark about my dancing. I listened, with my ears burning, while they took me apart. To Jan I was a creep and an awful bore. She went out with me, she admitted, because my grandfather was 'worth about a billion dollars.'"

Horgan paused and gave Barnes another twisted smile. "The other girl offered to take over. She said she thought she could become quite fond of a weirdo who was going to have that kind of money."

Barnes smiled sympathetically.

"I suppose I wasn't too bright, but you know this was the first time it really hit me—the phony relationships that can be precipitated by a pile of money. I mean, that a girl could dislike you intensely and yet let you make love to her, probably even marry her, just because you were going to be very rich one day."

Barnes shook his head. "I can understand how it might have been a traumatic experience."

Horgan glanced around the room, a little embarrassed at becoming carried away. "So you can understand why it's important to me," he said.

"Certainly. We'll say nothing."

"You haven't already told anyone here?"

"No. I think Lieutenant Shunk knows, but he's not the sort to volunteer information. Anyway, Ryan made it quite clear that this was to be kept absolutely confidential."

Horgan scraped his chair back and stood up. "Well, back to the mines. Thanks."

"Not at all," said Barnes. "No problem."

After Horgan left, closing the door, I said, "It's sure tough being rich."

He dismissed my flippancy with a faint smile.

"I promised Ryan I would be very discreet in dealing with Horgan." He stared thoughtfully into space for a few seconds. "I think we've been as discreet as we can be. Anyway, I'll handle him personally from now on. I want you to concentrate on Gates. Do some intensive research."

"You mean—"

"I mean tail him. I want to know everyone he meets or talks to outside this office."

If there is anything I hate, it's tailing. It's tedious, uncomfortable, and very tiring. However, I must face up to the fact that this is one of the ways I earn my bread.

"Okay," I said, sighing deeply. "But one guy can't tail in New York City."

"You'll work with Bill Perkes."

Another evening shot. The main activity would start after five, just when Isabel got off from work. How long would she stand for these lonely evenings without me? Oh well, it was better than being unemployed. Or selling encyclopedias.

Perkes showed up about nine-thirty, and we made the necessary arrangements. Perkes would wait in his rented car in the Consolidated parking lot, and I would cover Gates's leaving by the front door, on foot.

It was a very boring morning. I had to float around, keeping an eye on Gates's office and/or the front door. I mean, how long can you kid with a receptionist?

Finally, about twelve-thirty he decided to go out to lunch. While he was leaving by the front door I hurried out the back, signaled to Perkes, then ran around the building to the front. By that time Gates was far enough ahead for me to start after him. Perkes would follow with the car, in case Gates hailed a cab.

Gates headed for Madison Avenue, and I followed, a couple of hundred feet behind. Then he created a real problem for Perkes by sauntering into a large Chinese restaurant near Thirty-fourth Street. There was absolutely no place to park, of course, and the traffic was far too heavy to double-park. In less than ten minutes a squad car would be along.

When Perkes pulled alongside I said, "You'd better take the car back to Consolidated, come back here, and try to have a cab at the ready. Probably he's only going to eat lunch anyway."

Perkes nodded and drove off. At that moment a cab slid into a cab stand slot twenty feet south of the restaurant. I hurried across the street and got in.

"Where to?"

"Turn your meter on and sit here. I'm expecting a friend along shortly."

He turned around and gave me a hard look. "I got to write down a destination."

"When my friend arrives, we'll be headed uptown to the area around Rockefeller Center."

He stared at me suspiciously. At today's rates,

very few people get in a cab and ask the driver to turn the meter on and wait. With so many cabbie holdups and murders, you can't blame them for getting edgy about anything out of the ordinary.

I handed him five bucks. "Look, here's your tip in advance. I'm just trying to keep an eye on a guy. It's a simple divorce action. No violence."

"I ain't chasing nobody through traffic. No cops and robbers stuff, see."

"Relax. If we have to follow anyone it will only be a harmless John who's giving his wife fits. And there'll be twenty bucks more added to your tip."

He tucked the five away reluctantly, then settled down to read his *Daily News*.

I sat there watching the entrance and daydreaming about all the great Chinese food I could be eating while keeping an eye on Gates. Except that it wasn't practical. In a place that big and busy, the odds were that I would be too close to him, or too far away. In the meantime I could only think about sautéed shrimp with mushrooms and water chestnuts and drool. We'd probably have to snatch hot dogs somewhere on the run.

When Perkes joined me in about ten minutes it created another crisis with the cab driver. My friend had come and we were still asking to sit there with the meter running. Probably the other two members of our party were robbing the bank on the corner.

"Jeez, I wish you two guys would just get out. I'm here to *drive* people someplace, not just sit with the meter running."

Who could blame him? We were probably Mafia guys waiting to gun down somebody, and he, Aloysius Finnegan, would get nicked in the crossfire.

"For God's sake shut up," said Perkes. "We have legally engaged this cab, and if we want to sit here with the meter running, that's our prerogative."

I think using words like *legally engaged* and *prerogative* soothed him a little. He went back to reading his *Daily News,* but cocked around in his seat so he could keep an eye on us.

After all that hassle, Gates finally came out of the restaurant smug and stuffed, and marched right back to the office. You can see why I hate tailing.

The afternoon was equally miserable. Gates didn't go anywhere. I sent out for sandwiches and coffee, and posted myself at the door of an empty office near the steps on the second floor. To leave the building, Gates would have to pass me on the way down.

Late in the afternoon Perkes came in and we had a conference on how we would handle the "going home" situation. Gates had his car in the parking lot, but had said something about going home on the subway. Parking space being at a premium in Brooklyn Heights, it was possible that he kept his car in the Consolidated parking lot, only a short subway ride away if they needed it. If Gates took the subway home, I would follow on foot, also riding the subway, and Perkes would drive directly to Gates's apartment and wait there, if he could find anyplace to park. This is one reason tailing anybody in New York is so impossible. You need one guy in a car, and he's immobilized ninety percent of the time by traffic conditions and parking problems.

I like these stories where the hero just finds another cab immediately, steps in and says, "Follow that cab." In the first place, if the guy you are tailing grabs a cab, there isn't any other cab for you to grab. Ninety-nine percent of the time. The other one percent, the cabbie says, "Get the hell out of my cab, I'm calling the cops. I ain't following *nobody!*"

It was quarter of six when Gates decided to leave. He walked out the front door again, so I repeated my lunchtime maneuver, racing out the back, signaling Perkes, then running around the building to keep Gates in sight. Instead of heading for the subway, however, he started walking west.

At Fifth Avenue he turned north, and I had to move closer to keep him in sight. An old lady who was talking to herself came barging along, jostling everyone she met. She cut clear across the sidewalk to bump into me.

"Why don't you watch where you're going?" she screamed.

"Sorry," I said, trying to get by.

"You with your sheik sideburns. Rudolph Valentino you ain't!"

I ducked around her. Gates was getting too far ahead in the crowd.

"Mouse meat! You're a racist anthropologist!" she yelled after me.

Another one of the minor problems of tailing anybody in New York.

At Fifty-sixth Street he turned west again. About two-thirds of the way to Sixth Avenue he turned into a medium-priced French restaurant which happens to be pretty good. Isabel and I have eaten there many times. Tonight I would be dining from the Sabrett hot dog wagon across the street.

Perkes, who had managed to keep up with us by circling blocks and other maneuvers, pulled into a spot by a fireplug to rest while we talked.

"With or without sauerkraut?" I asked.

"Without. But plenty of mustard."

I bought four hot dogs and some Cokes. While we ate I picked out Gates's dinner for him, the pig. A big Chinese lunch, and now he was sitting in there eating a platter of assorted hors d'oeuvres, onion soup, stuffed lobster tails with a

136

carafe of white wine, salad, chocolate mousse, and filter coffee.

"Why doesn't this nit go home to his wife?" I asked Perkes.

"Maybe he doesn't like her cooking."

We sat there for an hour and a half while he gorged himself. I made two sneaky trips into the restaurant to see whether he was alone or meeting someone we should know about. Both times he was enjoying his food unaccompanied.

Leaving the restaurant, he strolled to Sixth and headed south. All the way to Forty-second Street. Some walker. He paused for a moment in front of a pornographic movie, considered it carefully, and then decided to go in.

Perkes pulled up. "You'd better take the car back to Consolidated," I said, "and try to get back here in an hour with a cab."

I bought a ticket and went in. Four dollars. It was difficult locating Gates in the dark. My carrot consumption has been low in recent months. Eventually I spotted his white hair about half-way down, and found a seat several rows behind him.

The film was very low in redeeming social values. It consisted almost entirely of close-ups, in full color, of sex organs copulating. I think there were some people involved who belonged to the sex organs on display, but they had very minor roles in the production. The first five min-

137

utes stimulated a certain amount of clinical interest on my part, since I had never looked at a girl with a magnifying glass. After that it began to get monotonous, and I was glad the four dollars was on expense account. After my eyes became accustomed to the dark, I looked around. The audience was entirely male, and surprisingly, mostly young men. I would have guessed that this show's appeal would be to the middle-aged, frustrated, and sex-starved.

While I was surveying the audience a young black wearing jeans and a moderate Afro haircut came down the aisle and eased into the seat next to Gates. In a moment Gates tilted his head slightly, as though listening to something the Afro haircut said.

Was this a prearranged meeting? Or was the Afro merely doing a little pimping, or begging? He remained there about ten minutes, and Gates's head inclined slightly several more times. Either it was a meeting or Gates was being hustled. A plea for money wouldn't be all that interesting.

Several minutes after the black left, Gates got up and made for the exit. Outside the Afro was talking to a young Negro girl with yellow hair. She was dressed in boots, hot pants, and a see-through blouse, and looked like one of the girls working the streets. Gates joined them while I peeked through the glass door from the lobby.

Their session was over in seconds, Gates

turning to head in one direction and the two blacks walking off in the other. Either the price was wrong, or Gates had been oversold.

I had thought he would stay in the movie at least an hour, but the whole time elapsed was only twenty-five minutes. Understandably, Perkes had not returned. But for once I got a break. Gates went straight home by subway.

I have a few master keys that work on apartment lobby doors. After Gates had time to get up to his apartment I crossed the street and tried a couple, the second one working. I took the elevator to the fifth floor, and moved quietly to the door labeled 5-G. There was nothing but the television blaring, then suddenly it was turned off.

"Hard day at the glue factory, dear?" asked a female voice.

"The usual."

"Hungry?"

"No, I had a couple of sandwiches sent in. I'm going to have a drink, look at the paper, and then hit the sack."

Some sandwiches he had sent in. At least it was only nine-fifteen, early enough to see Isabel. I headed downstairs in a hurry, and double-timed to the subway.

Isabel has long straight blond hair which reaches to her waist, a figure that is provocative to say the least, and a face that I love. She is also motivated by white-hot idealism. We are plotting to get married eventually, when we get time between recycling paper and bottles, and settling some of the grave injustices rampant in the world. My theory is that we should save enough money to cop out for a year in some cheap seacoast place in Italy or Spain. Of course, I don't know how Barnes will get along without me.

"I don't see why you have to work every night," said Isabel, "I had to carry a ton of papers downstairs all by myself, and take a cab to a recycling depot. And it cost three dollars and sixty-five cents."

If I had been there, it would have cost *me* three dollars and sixty-five cents for the cab fare. The way she throws money around on cab fares, we'll never get to Italy.

I told her about my evening, how I only got two lousy hot dogs for dinner, and had to tail the subject into a boring pornographic movie, then take two subway rides, and so on. Then I told her about the day before, particularly my duel with Spinoza McWilliams.

She just stared at me with her big blue eyes, probably thinking that I'm making half of it up. "Would you like some canned beans and hot dogs?" she asked.

"Hot dogs. Ugh."

"Well, we could go out for a pizza."

"For pizza we could go over to my place," I said. Her place is short on privacy because of her apartment mate, Kathy. Kathy is a born loser and spends entirely too much time around the apartment, usually getting over some boy who has done her wrong. Psychologically it's bad for us. Every time Kathy goes through one of her periodic weeping, screaming, I-don't-care-if-I-live-or-not sessions following her discovery that her current boyfriend is married and has two kids, I can sense a hardening of Isabel's attitude toward me. I mean, she doesn't become hostile. Just wary.

"I'm too tired to go way over to your place," she said.

"Kathy in trouble again?"

"How did *you* know?"

"ESP."

"We could take some bottles to the recycling depot."

"That will be a thrill."

We went to a restaurant nearby and had pizza and red wine, then went back to Isabel's apartment and studied our joint savings account book, which had one thousand thirty-five dollars and eighty-six cents in it. Kathy stayed in the bedroom, giving forth muffled wails from time to time.

Some evening.

The next two days were even worse. The most boring two days I have ever had in my life. Gates went nowhere that he shouldn't be, but he was very active, visiting a lot of stores, which probably had some problems with Consolidated money orders. From my brief sessions with

Barnes, I gathered that Tip had done nothing unusual either, and had been scrupulously staying away from the Village. I wondered if we were not wasting our time.

"What's Shunk doing?" I asked Barnes. "Why doesn't he have his men do all this boring tailing?"

Barnes smiled. "Short-handed. For him, this case is only one of several. Anyway, he's concentrating on Cressett's contacts."

"How long do we have to keep this up?"

"Do you have any better ideas?"

I thought about that long and carefully. Almost anything was preferable to dodging around behind Gates for days on end. "Has Tony Wilson developed anything new on Cressett?" Harry Weiner had been working with Barnes tailing Tip Horgan.

"Nothing."

"What about Ryan?"

"Shunk is checking out Ryan."

I had to admit that I couldn't think of anything better to do.

The next day Perkes and I decided to give up using the car. Traffic and parking problems made it virtually useless anyway. We'd both work on foot and depend on that fragile reed, a cab, in an emergency. Unsatisfactory, but what else can you do in midtown Manhattan?

Instead of going home, Gates headed across

town again, and dined splendidly in my favorite French restaurant. We waited down the block, eating hot dogs. If this routine kept up, I'd soon be living on Pepto-Bismol the way Barnes does.

When he finally came out, he walked west to the Avenue of the Americas and then started downtown at a fast clip. Needed to shake down all the bouillabaisse and crêpes suzette he had been gorging

Perkes took the other side of the street and I followed directly behind Gates. Between Forty-ninth and Forty-fifth I had to do a lot of dodging of girls with dubious propositions. "Sorry, no money. Flat broke. No bread," I said, weaving past one after another. One offered me credit on my Everywhere Charge card, and I almost lost sight of Gates trying to get around her.

At Forty-fourth he turned east and we hiked across town to the Vanderbilt Avenue entrance of Grand Central Station. This entrance puts you on a balcony overlooking the main concourse, with a wide divided staircase flowing down to the upper level. There's another large concourse below it, known as the lower level, in case you've never been in Grand Central.

Since Gates was about two hundred feet ahead of me, he had already negotiated the steps when I got to the balcony, and was headed straight for the circular information booth in the center of the station. A standard meeting place. I waited.

Down there he had a number of choices. He could head for the Forty-second Street exits, the Lexington Avenue exits, turn back past the steps and up the ramp to Vanderbilt Avenue and Forty-second Street, or he could come back up the steps past me. He could also take a tunnel to the Roosevelt Hotel at Forty-fifth and Madison. There were a couple of dozen other options open. He could take a train to Westchester or Connecticut, or a subway to almost anywhere. I could watch his next move from the balcony almost as easily as dodging around through the light crowd.

He stopped at the information booth, looked around, then looked at his watch. Perkes came up beside me.

"He's meeting someone," I said. "Over by the information booth."

Perkes searched the scattered crowd and located him.

Gates paced ten steps one way, then turned and paced back. He lit a cigarette and stood impatiently puffing it. In three minutes he stamped it out and resumed his walk, this time circling the booth.

"She's late," said Perkes.

"Yeah, I wonder—" I broke off. I suddenly saw who Gates was meeting. Spinoza McWilliams. You couldn't miss that flying-V hairdo from a mile away. He was sauntering toward Gates from the Lexington Avenue end of the station, sharply resplendent in a bright-blue blazer, white turtleneck shirt, red and gray striped bell-bottoms.

Spinoza looked taller than he should be, which was strange, because I was looking down on him. He was probably wearing the new four-inch heels.

They didn't shake hands on meeting. They seemed to just sort of stare at each other. Gates lit another cigarette and they began to talk animatedly. In a situation like this it would be great if you had field glasses and could read lips. Since neither was available, equipment or lip-reading talent, I could only guess from posture and set of shoulders, and a few hand movements, that they were arguing. When Gates started poking Spinoza in the chest with his forefinger I was sure of it. On the last poke, Spinoza brushed Gates's finger away angrily and they just glared at each other for a few seconds.

I had a decision to make. When they parted, Perkes and I should split, covering both parties, since Spinoza was obviously tied in with the case. As Barnes's left-hand man, I was calling the shots on these expeditions. The easy way out for me would be to say to Perkes, "You take McWilliams, I'll follow Gates." I didn't want to have anything more to do with Spinoza McWilliams. He was probably head of the whole

Black Mafia in Harlem, and he had already kissed me on the cheek, so to speak. I was marked to become extinct. On the other hand, it was cowardly. Craven. So it's craven, I said to myself, I'm cravin' not to meet up with Spinoza McWilliams *no more!* Perkes wouldn't be in as much danger. He hadn't been marked for extinction.

"When and if they separate, you take Gates, and I'll follow the black guy," I said, cautiously feeling the bulge of my .38, which I had worn faithfully ever since my afternoon of the blades. "I know him and some of his associates."

Something to do with the conditioning I got from my backsliding Presbyterian father, I suppose. If you're afraid of something, you've just got to be a stupid idiot and tackle it.

Gates held out his hand to McWilliams, and McWilliams responded, reaching for it. There was a very brief and tiny glint of metal as something small passed from Gates to Spinoza. Spinoza turned quickly on one of his four-inch heels and started in the direction of the balcony. Gates headed for Forty-second Street.

"Well, see you," I said to Perkes, resisting an impulse to order a last-minute switch of jobs.

Perkes wisely hurried out of the Vanderbilt Avenue entrance, from which he could zip down to Forty-second Street and be waiting for Gates to emerge a hundred or so feet east of him.

I waited until Spinoza made his way under the balcony to the left of me, then galloped down the steps two at a time. He was walking jauntily down the ramp to the lower level. I followed cautiously, keeping a nervous eye out for any Afro haircuts that might be escorting him from a distance.

On the lower level he started walking east across the concourse, keeping near the side with the track gates. Fortunately there was a fairly large crowd waiting for a late-leaving Stamford local, which was probably waiting for another engine, and I could keep closer behind him without being seen. As we approached the corridor leading to the steps at the northeast end of the concourse, he slowed to a creep and began to look at the numbers on the metal lockers lining the walls. Now I knew what Gates had given him. A key, of course.

A party of seven tall Scandinavian tourists, e tan and blond and carrying SAS flight bags, gave me an opportunity to move in closer. I edged into the middle of the group as we approached Spinoza. He had found the right locker, and he glanced quickly around before bending to open it. Apparently he saw nothing suspicious about us Swedes. The locker in question was the bottom one, flush with the floor. He opened the door and started pulling out a suitcase, about a two-suiter size. Consolidated's money? I doubted that he was going to Darien for the weekend. If I tracked him to Harlem, I would be badly out numbered. On impulse I drifted to the back of the group and, as they went by, stepped quickly up to Spinoza's bent form and shoved my .38 in his back.

6

"Okay, Spinoza," I said, "you and I and the suit-case go to the nearest police station." I reached for the handle and tried to force his fingers out of it. He straightened up, still holding it.

"Whitey, you completely out of your mind."

"I'm not whitey, I'm your ex-friend Larry Howe."

"Whoever you are, let go of my suitcase," he said over his shoulder.

I jerked the suitcase, keeping the barrel of the .38 hard against his back. He wouldn't let go. Then I heard the clatter of leather shoes on the marble, running toward us. It was Abdul, his bushy ball of hair making him at least seven feet tall. I swung back to the lockers.

Spinoza let go of the handle and reached into his jacket pocket quickly. There was a click, and his switchblade was open, all six inches of its ra-zor sharpness.

"Shoot me and I cut your stomach out before I die!"

"Cut me and I'll blow your head off before I die. And that goes for Abdul too." He was now about ten feet away and had slowed to a walk, aware of the knife and the gun.

We stared at each other, hate oozing out of our pores almost visibly. There was only one thing to do. I started to yell at the top of my lungs. "Help! Help! I'm being mugged! Help! Help! Get the police! Help!"

Both Spinoza and Abdul glanced around nervously. In a fraction of a second I whipped the revolver upward, fired a shot, and had it back pointing in their direction before either made a move. I was getting hoarse, but I kept yelling, "Help! Robbery! Get the police!"

"Harvey Motherbanger, you cut out that noise," said Abdul, "Or I going to break every bone in your body, even the ones in your little toe."

I yelled louder, if that was possible.

"Let's cut out of here," said Spinoza. He turned and started toward the steps in a trot.

I fired another shot in the air and kept on yelling. Abdul turned and ran after Spinoza.

I kept yelling, just in case.

When they were out of sight I put the .38 back in its holster, just before one of the station cops hove into view.

"What's going on here?"

"A couple of blacks tried to snatch my suitcase. They went that way, up the steps."

"Sounded like somebody shooting."

150

"One's about seven foot tall with an Afro hair-cut, the other's short, wearing a blue blazer." I pointed to the steps. "They're only about ten seconds ahead of you."

"You stay here," he said, and ran toward the steps.

I walked off in the other direction quickly, lugging the suitcase, which was heavy enough to contain the entire loot from the robbery. I was embarrassed about the shooting. Bullets ricocheting off a ceiling can hurt somebody. The truth is I was in a panic, because I didn't know whether I would be able to shoot Spinoza and Abdul if they tried to close in on me. Even though I had been in Vietnam, I was never forced to shoot anyone. They say you never know whether you can until you have to.

At the Vanderbilt Avenue entrance I popped into a cab. It only took us about twenty minutes to creep through traffic to the safety of Consolidated's offices. I made the cab driver very nervous by continually surveying every car on both sides and behind us. Spinoza would hardly have had time to catch up with me, but he might have lucked out by taking a wild chance. He could have grabbed a cab on Lexington, circled around to get to Vanderbilt, covering the Forty-second Street exits on the way.

"You need to go to the bathroom or something, mister?" the cab driver asked.

"No," I said, "you got ants back here."

He turned to give me a raised-eyebrow look, and almost bumped the cab directly ahead of us.

I carried the suitcase up to the conference room. Barnes, Shunk, and Ryan were sitting there yakking. I wondered if Barnes had given up on Horgan. It was only eight o'clock.

Shunk eyed the suitcase. "What you got there, more encyclopedias?"

I hoisted it up onto the conference table. "I just hijacked this suitcase from Spinoza McWilliams."

I told them about Gates's meeting with Spinoza, and my subsequent encounter. "Since he wouldn't go to the police station with me to open it, I can only assume it contains the money, or dope. If it's dope, you'd better put me on the first plane to Australia, because I'm emigrating."

All three had been listening with intent interest. "For Christ's sake," said Ryan, "Dave Gates—"

Shunk, who had been staring open-mouthed, came to and said, "Well, let's open the bugger." He came around the table, flipped the latches at both ends, and threw the lid back. A sheet of old newspaper blanketed the contents. Shunk pulled the tucked edges loose and removed it. Money. Neat stacks of green with white bands holding the bills into packages about an inch thick.

Ryan came over from the other side of the table and stared. Then he stomped over to the window and turned his back on us, ostensibly looking out the window. Very upset about Gates, I imagined.

Shunk dumped the contents of the suitcase onto the table and we made a quick count. Nothing but ten-dollar bills. Forty packages of two hundred and fifty tens. One hundred thousand dollars. Where was the other four hundred thousand?

Ryan turned and came back to the table. "The fact that you saw Dave Gates meet Spinoza McWilliams doesn't prove anything whatsoever with regard to his having anything to do with this money," he said.

"I saw him pass a key to McWilliams."

"Could you swear in court that it was a key you saw? From that distance?"

"No."

Shunk said, "We'll have to see what Gates says about all this." He picked up the conference-room phone and called his office, issuing instructions for Gates to be picked up.

I knew they had some serial numbers identifying the robbery money, but not all. When Shunk put the telephone down I asked, "I suppose the serial numbers you have are only for the larger denominations?"

Shunk nodded. "Only the fifties and hundreds."

Ryan picked up one of the packages and flipped the bills contemptuously. "Dave Gates wouldn't have had anything to do with this. What you've hijacked is probably Mafia money. I hope you've got plenty of life insurance."

A small cold wind drifted down my spine, which was probably turning one of the lighter shades of yellow. "They'll know it was a mistake," I said. "They'll know I'm not the type of guy who goes around hijacking the Mafia."

Ryan sneered. "Personally, I wouldn't bet a worn-out tennis shoe on your chances."

Barnes, who was smiling grimly, consulted his cigarette notebook. Completing his ritual, he lit one and said, "If Dave Gates had nothing to do with this money, it is certainly one of the strangest coincidences I have ever encountered."

"Bull," said Ryan. "Dave's meeting with McWilliams was probably purely by accident. The fact that McWilliams is some kind of bag man has nothing to do with Dave."

"Purely by accident? He waited almost ten minutes for McWilliams to arrive. They talked and then separated. It was obviously a prearranged meeting," I said.

Ryan glared at me. "You—" he said, then turned on his heel and stomped out.

"Very strange," said Barnes.

Shunk's eyebrows were riding high. "Yeah," he said, "funny—"

Perkes drifted in, with his lower lip drooping.

Either he had lost Gates or Gates was back in the building. From the look on his face, I gathered that it was the former.

"Where did you lose him?"

"In Grand Central, dammit. He didn't come out the Forty-second Street exit he was headed for. I doubled back into the station, but by then he was gone."

"Did you look in the drugstore? The big Liggett's?"

"Does that have an entrance into the station?"

I nodded. There was no point in postmorteming. Tailing anyone in Manhattan was impossible, anyway. Overground and underground the buildings have so many entrances and corridors leading to other buildings. On a rainy day, for instance, you can go underground all the way from Forty-first Street and Lexington to Fifty-first and Sixth Avenue, four long crosstown blocks and ten shorter uptown blocks. You have to surface briefly a couple of times to do this, but you are indoors ninety-eight percent of the way.

"Don't worry," said Shunk. "We'll have Mr. Gates muy pronto."

Perkes was staring pop-eyed at the open suitcase. I told him about Spinoza McWilliams and could see a tinge of green envy creeping up his face. Little did he know, I would almost have traded the honor and glory of my spectacular coup for the security of having Spinoza after Perkes instead of me.

"You might as well call it a night, Bill," said Barnes.

He pays Perkes, Wilson, and Weiner by the hour, so he doesn't keep them around on a whim the way he does me.

Perkes said good night and left.

"Larry, let's go across the street and talk to the Preeble woman," said Barnes.

Preeble? For a few seconds I couldn't place the name. She was the witness who didn't see anything.

"I doubt if you'll get anything from that dumb broad," said Shunk.

"No harm in trying," said Barnes.

On our way out of the building I said, "Ryan was sure doing a real burn over my report. *Very* peculiar. Could it be that he and Gates are in this together?"

Barnes shrugged. "His attitude was certainly strange, I'll agree."

Doris Preeble was a fairly attractive brunette of about twenty-five. She was dressed in a short, thigh-length shift, which could have been a nightgown or a dress. Who knows?

Barnes explained our mission. She gave us a careful once over and then said, "Come in, I guess."

The small living room was furnished with old,

nondescript plush upholstered furniture and a very large boyfriend. On the stout side, he was about six feet tall and balding. He was puffing on a badly chewed up cigar and didn't bother to get up.

"This is my friend Mr. McQueeg," she said, introducing us.

We nodded. No one was shaking hands on this one.

"Don't get involved, doll," said McQueeg.

"How can I get involved? I didn't see anything." Her voice had a faint whine, and I had the impression she was dissappointed that she couldn't report something sensational, like the robbers turning and staring right up at her.

McQueeg shifted the cigar to the other side of his mouth without hands. Quite a feat. It was done with neat tongue work and fast contortions of his fat lips. "Doll, the best thing is not to get involved. It don't pay."

"We don't want to involve you in anything unpleasant, Miss Preeble," said Barnes. "We'd just like to verify certain aspects of your statement to the police."

"I didn't see nothing. If I seen anything, I'd be glad to tell you."

"It don't pay," said McQueeg. "I was a witness in a case where a guy was hit in the eye by a hot pastrami sandwich thrown by a cook, causing certain injuries to the gent'man's eye. They wasn't able to ascertain the extent of the injuries, if there was any, and nobody got nuthin. I lost three days from work."

"Like you say, it don't pay to get involved," said Doris.

McQueeg stood up. His blue shirt was so tight across his stomach that white patches of undershirt showed between buttons.

"Doll, I got to go to work." He looked at Barnes. "I'll see you gent'man out. Doris here didn't see nuthin. She ain't involved."

"Honest, I wish I could tell you something, but what can I say?" asked Doris.

The docile way in which Barnes allowed McQueeg to usher us out could only mean that we'd be coming back. Barnes never gives up until he has the full story, no matter how futile it may seem.

We left, walked across the street to Consolidated's lobby, and watched through the heavy glass doors until we saw McQueeg leave, which occurred in about five minutes. We gave him another five minutes to get well away from the apartment, and then went back.

"Oh, hi," said Doris, "Forget something?"

Barnes smiled. "May we come in a moment? There are a couple of things I meant to ask."

She opened the door wider. "Sure. I got time." With McQueeg gone, she was much friendlier. Probably lonely.

In the living room she asked, "You want coffee? I was just making a pot."

"That's very kind of you. I'd like very much to have a cup," said Barnes.

While she was in the kitchen, we strolled over to her front windows and studied the street below. The lights above Consolidated's entrance illuminated that side of the street fairly well. The sidewalk bordering the apartment house was in deep shadow. The nearest streetlight s about fifty yards away, near Madison Avenue.

"If she were looking, she'd certainly have a good view of anything entering or leaving," said Barnes.

"*If* she were looking."

"Hmmmmm."

Doris returned, carrying a tray with coffeepot, cups, and a platter containing a sliced pound cake.

"I made the cake myself."

"Looks delicious," I said.

She giggled. "Wait'll you try it. It's probably *horrible*."

We occupied ourselves with cream, sugar, and cake for several minutes, telling her how great the cake was.

"The evening of the robbery—"said Barnes.

"Say, wasn't that some robbery!" she interrupted. "I was shocked, I mean *shocked*. And they killed that poor man! I'm afraid to go out of the apartment after dark."

"You were—"

"As I was saying to Mac, you just don't know where you can go to be safe these days. Mac, you met him, he's a bartender and he can tell you some stories that would make your hair stand on end."

"About the evening of the robbery—"

"I was in the subway the other day and this little girl come up to me. She couldn't have been more than ten years old. She said, 'Miss, I'm so hungry. Would you give me a quarter to get a hot dog?' Well, I was reaching in my pocketbook for my change purse, and would you *believe* what this ten-year-old did? She snatched my purse. Tried to yank it right away from me. I yanked it back, and she hauled off and hit me. Right here." Doris pointed to her ample bosom. "I mean, it hurt like anything."

Barnes sighed sympathetically, then sipped his coffee.

"I carry a pair of scissors in my purse. Everywhere." She produced her pocketbook, which had been tucked down in one corner of the sofa, and fished out her shears, which were thin, with blades about eight inches long.

I was afraid Barnes might settle down to a lecture on the danger of this type of weapon, but for once he seemed a bit nonplussed.

160

"I wonder—" he started, but she was off again before he could get a third word in.

"I was at this sale in Gimbels. They had some really lovely bedspreads for about *one third* what they usually sell for. So I bought several. One sort of pastel blue, a pink one, and one sort of creamy yellow. Well, when I was walking back on Thirty-sixth Street, this nice-looking little man came up to me and asked me if I could direct him to some address in Brooklyn. He showed me this piece of paper with an address on it, and while I was trying to explain about not knowing Brooklyn that well, he snatched my package of bedspreads and ran off. Mac was furious, because he had given me the money for the bedspreads. And Mac does like a pretty bed." She stopped suddenly and made a small "o" of her lips, like a little girl who realizes she has said something naughty.

She recovered and smiled, took a deep breath, and continued. "Mac. Mac had the batt'ry stolen right out of his car. He says to himself, 'Well, they didn't get such a good deal. The batt'ry was three and a half years old and getting weaker every day. So he's going to have go buy a new batt'ry anyway. Would you *believe*, the very first night they came and took the new batt'ry and put the old one back in his car!"

Barnes rolled his eyes upward and I made appropriate sounds of disbelief.

"Tell us about the night of the robbery," Barnes said loudly and desperately.

About to launch another episode, she stopped, mouth open. "What do you mean?"

"Try to remember everything that happened that evening. The times you were looking out the front windows, any noises you might have heard, anything at all."

"I don't see—"

"Little things that may seem completely unimportant to you can provide important clues for an investigator."

"You mean, like a detective on television? I saw this show the other night, this guy was sort of a foreign agent and—"

Barnes lit a cigarette without consulting his notebook, he was so upset. We waited patiently while she unwound the television half hour, scene by scene.

When she reached the end, she was obviously as confused as we were about who did what. Barnes said, "Think about the evening of the robbery as if it were a television show. You're the heroine sitting over here in her apartment. Across the street more than a half million dollars is being stolen by armed robbers ready for violence. They murder a guard and leave. Now, the side door leading to the parking lot was double-bolted from the inside. The robbers probably entered through the front door, and they certainly *had* to leave through the front door. This

162

action had to take place less that fifty feet from your windows. There was probably a car waiting with the motor running. When they ran out to enter the car, the driver probably gunned the motor up loudly for a fast takeoff. Later there were probably police sirens and, if I remember correctly, about four squad cars with red lights revolving. There were people going in and out. Police, myself, and Larry here." He paused for breath, because he had been speaking very rapidly to ward off interruption. "Tell us what the heroine of our little drama was doing all this time."

She had been listening with her mouth open slightly.

"Gee," she said, and was silent for a few seconds. "It sounds so exciting, and I missed everything."

"Tell us about how you spent the evening anyway. Some little thing may provide us important information."

The getaway car could have been waiting in the parking lot, and probably was, because someone had taken time to put the small packet of money in Cressett's car, but Barnes was trying to stimulate her with drama, and it made a more exciting picture for her this way.

"Gee," she said, "I don't see how it'll help, but I'll try. Lemme see. Mac was on the nine-to-two shift at the bar. I washed some of his shirts and pressed them. He don't like the way the China-

163

man does them any more. Then I watched television until I got tired. I guess that was after twelve. So then I made myself a little snack. A cheeseburger with coffee. Oh yes, I had some sliced tomatoes with it, and a little piece of cake after. Then I remember looking at my watch, because I figured Mac might be coming along soon, because if there's no action they close the bar up early, and he gets home maybe one-fifteen or one-thirty. If there's action, he don't get home until maybe two-thirty. So when I looked at my watch it was maybe one-fifteen. So, I'm sitting there in the front window looking for him to come along. He always walks over on the other side of the street, because it's better lighted, and who knows when somebody is going to jump out of a dark doorway and mug you."

Barnes's eyebrows had been getting steadily higher. "What time did Mac get home?"

Her eyes widened. "He didn't. Would you *believe*, his sister was taken ill with acute appendicitis. He had to leave the bar about twelve and get an ambulance to take her to the hospital."

We made sympathetic sounds. "So you were watching for Mac. Until when?"

"Oh, I saw the police cars come. That must have been after two. Believe me, there was no robbers that left, like you said. They must have done it before one-fifteen."

"And you were watching the whole time? Between one-fifteen and the time the police cars arrived?"

She nodded. "I like to see Mac coming. It's so scary when you hear footsteps coming up the stairs and you don't know who it might be. When I see Mac across the street I go and take the chain off the door."

"You saw *no one* enter or leave Consolidated?"

"Well, there was a gent'man that left, but he wasn't no robber. He works there. I seen him before."

"What time was this?"

"Maybe five minutes before the police came."

"You definitely recognized him?"

She thought about it, pursing her lips. "Well, like, I didn't see his face. His build just looked familiar. Then, he locked the door when he left, and he wouldn't have done that if he was a robber. Also, he wasn't carrying nothing." She giggled. "You can't put a half million dollars in your coat pocket. Believe me, he wasn't no robber. He locked the door and then strolled off down the street toward Lexington. No hurry."

"Why didn't you tell this to the police?"

She stared at him blankly. "I didn't think of it. The gent'man *works* there. I didn't think his leaving had anything to do with the robbers. People that work there leave late at night all the time. I see them when I'm watching for Mac."

From her description of the late leaver's build,

it could have been Gates, Horgan, or even Cressett. It could have been Ryan but for the fact that he had called the police, and was there when they arrived.

"You're certain he was carrying nothing?"

She nodded. "After he locked the door, he lit a cigarette. If he had been carrying anything, he would have had to put it down. Anything big, I mean."

For a dum-dum, she had a pretty good memory.

"I mean, really, if you had just robbed a place, you wouldn't step right outside and light a cigarette, would you?" Some of Barnes's concern at her not reporting the incident had gotten through and she was trying to justify her oversight. "He even walked down the street swinging his arms, like some people do. I definitely remember."

We thanked her for the coffee and cake and left. The poor girl would be in for quite a going over from Shunk and his men.

If the robbery had occurred before one-fifteen, then Ryan was either lying or very confused. He claimed that he had visited the vault about one-thirty, expecting the Denzer mechanics any minute. It seems that they were required to go through a rather complicated identification dance before being admitted, for obvious reasons. Ryan was the only executive present who had all the codes and passwords necessary to test the identification. According to his story, he had chatted with Wicher for a couple of minutes, then returned to his office, having decided that it was useless to wait downstairs. Impatience had driven him there, but it still might be a half hour or so before they arrived.

If Ryan was lying, it fitted well with my theory that he and Gates were tied in together.

When we reached the sidewalk I asked Barnes, "Where to now?"

"I wonder if Shunk is still there," he said, eyeing the Consolidated building. He looked at me. "If you want to knock off, go ahead. It's been a long day."

I was curious to see what Shunk would say about our newest revelation and followed him across the street without answering. Tomlinson, the night watchman, substitutes as sort of door orderly while anyone is still working at night. Recognizing us, he unlocked the door and let us in.

"Lieutenant Shunk still up there?"

"Nope."

"Mr. Ryan?"

"Yep."

Barnes headed for the stairs. "I wanted to see Shunk," he muttered as I followed him up the steps.

Ryan was at his desk, shuffling papers. He looked up. "Oh, Berk, glad you came back. We've got to have a talk. Sit down."

We sat. Ryan lit a cigarette, his hand trembling slightly. "I'll make it brief. I've got to take you off this job. I'm getting too much flak from up above. The General isn't satisfied with the progress we've been making."

"Oh?" said Barnes. I felt in my pocket for the Pepto-Bismol.

"It's probably more serious than you realize. The newspapers haven't said much about the inside-job angle, but the word must be getting around. One of our biggest supermarket chains switched to American Express the other day without any warning or explanation. Today, one of our biggest drug chain customers asked us to forward our latest financial statement. We've got to have action and *fast*."

"Oh." This time I said it, and wasn't a question, but more a cry of pain.

"National Group is taking over as of immediately. Now, Berk, I don't want you to think this is going to hurt our relationship. We'll be calling on you in the future, I'm sure. This particular job is just too big for your organization. You don't have the resources."

National Group was certainly big, all right, but I wondered if maybe Tip Horgan hadn't shafted us with the old man. Or maybe Ryan thought we were getting too close for comfort.

Barnes made a note of it, and then lit a cigarette. "Well, Rod," he said, "I don't agree that we haven't given you plenty of action. However, you and General Ellsworth have apparently made your decision, and I suppose there is nothing I can do about it."

"I'm not saying you haven't done a competent job, Berk. In a way, you're sort of a victim of our panic. The old man wants immediate results. I've got to make some kind of dramatic move. The only thing I can think of is to call in a bigger army."

Barnes puffed on his cigarette thoughtfully. "You're going to waste a lot of time while they cover much of the same ground we've already covered."

Ryan shrugged. He stood up and held out his hand. "Let's keep in touch. This isn't the last time we'll be doing business, I'm sure."

They shook hands, then Ryan dismissed me also with a brief wave of his hand as he sat down and began shuffling his papers again.

Out on the sidewalk I handed Barnes the small bottle of Pepto-Bismol. He threw it very hard into one of the city's wastepaper receptacles, where it cracked against the wire side and spilled pink goo all over the accumulated debris.

"Maybe you'd like a couple of Gelusil tablets?"

He turned on me, teeth bared. Then he relaxed and smiled. "Larry, we've been working long hours under a lot of tension. Let's take a little holiday."

"Okay," I said. "Shouldn't we see Shunk and tell him about Doris Preeble?" As much as I hate long hours and having my relationship with Isabel interfered with, I resented being cut off from the case. You get interested, and this was the first time I had ever seen Barnes fail to wrap up a case.

"Take tomorrow off," he said. "I'll call Shunk when I get home."

Tomorrow off. From the way he was talking, I thought he was going to give me at least a week. One day off. Big deal.

As though reading my mind he said, "Well, maybe two days. We have that Long Island outfit on the docket. Beekly Corporation?"

"Beerly Corporation." They had a problem with massive pilferage. It had been going on for months, so they could wait another day all right.

Though it was only ten o'clock, the subway platform was completely deserted. I suddenly remembered that I was marked for extinction by the Black Mafia, or whatever it was that Spinoza McWilliams headed. Not only was I marked for extinction, but I had incurred an extra hundred thousand dollars' worth of unbridled hostility. I backed up to one wall put one hand inside my jacket and grasped the butt of my .38, and remained in this somewhat odd position, swiveling my head from left to right and back until the train pulled in. The car I got on was sparsely populated. There were three Afro haircuts at the other end, but they paid no attention to me. I remained stationed at the empty end, my hand still tucked in my jacket clutching the Smith & Wesson. Reasonably innocent-looking types got on and off at the few stops before my street, but I managed to keep good armswinging distance from them all, and to position myself so that no one could get behind me. It's hard to get your back to the wall in a subway train, but I managed it by standing against a set of doors on the opposite side of the train from the platforms, which open only at express stops.

The area around my apartment would be especially dangerous, of course, because Spinoza wouldn't have to do too much detective work to find out where I lived.

Leaving the subway, I proceeded with great caution. It took me about ten minutes to walk the three blocks from the subway stop to my street. I tried to keep at least fifty feet between myself and any suspicious-looking pedestrians, especially those loitering or window shopping, and especially the two with the Afro haircuts walking about a hundred feet ahead of me. Also I had to keep a wary eye out for slow-moving cars. I crossed and recrossed the street at least six times, I gave every doorway careful scrutiny before passing, and if anyone behind me approached walking rapidly, I stopped and faced him, pretending to look for street numbers.

At the corner of York Avenue and my street in the seventies I stopped for a good three minutes just to look. In the hundred and fifty feet between the corner and my apartment building there was no one but a girl walking a dog. It was too dark to tell about doorways, across the street and on my side. I moved a few feet down the street and waited some more. No movement. I walked another twenty feet and eased into an empty apartment foyer. I stood there another five minutes, searching the other side of the street. No movement that I could see, but it was too dark to be sure.

Keeping close to the curb, I walked another fifty feet, then eased into another empty doorway. At this point the block was completely empty, except for a small tiger-striped cat rubbing against my leg and purring. I bent over and scratched its neck.

Maybe I was overdoing it. The cat and I were probably alone on the block. The time elapsed between my hijacking of Spinoza's suitcase and now, two hours plus, was short. But finding my address would require no time at all. Spinoza was certainly bright enough not to overlook the obvious. I was listed in the New York telephone directory. I would have to think about getting an unlisted number.

I moved carefully out of the doorway, scanning the doorways across the street and ahead on my side. A match flared briefly in an entranceway across the street from my own. Just about enough to light a cigarette. I waited. If it was a legitimate inhabitant pausing to light up before leaving the building, he should be showing himself. He didn't. Of course, it could be a couple talking. I cautiously strolled another twenty feet, stopping in another doorway where I waited and watched. A cab with off-duty lights on approached from the opposite direction. As it went by the entranceway in question I stared hard. The headlights didn't provide much help, but I was certain that I caught a brief glimpse of a couple of towering Afro haircuts.

Panic. They were waiting for me. Had they seen me approaching? Probably not. Wouldn't have lit a cigarette. On the other hand, they could have caught sight of me *after* lighting up. Looking over my shoulder, I moved out of the doorway and started walking quietly back toward York Avenue. The two Afro haircuts came out of the entrance way and started trotting in my direction. One was certainly tall enough to be Abdul.

I started running. This far up, York Avenue would be almost as deserted as my street. I hoped neither of them were track stars.

"Harvey! We just want to talk to you!" yelled one of them.

I kept running. At York Avenue they were still about a hundred feet behind me. I headed downtown and lengthened my stride for a long-distance sprint. You can't look backward and run efficiently, so I covered another block without looking back, running as fast and hard as

173

I've ever run in my life. I've never been chased by anyone out to kill me before. There's nothing like motivation to improve performance. I was flying, man.

At the corner, the light was against me, but I continued on anyhow, almost running into a Volkswagen. A quick broken field dodge around the rear fenders put me right in the path of a cab roaring through from the other direction. I made a mighty leap for the curb and was missed by inches, recovered, and pounded on down the block.

A squad car pulled up ahead of me, the door flipped open, and out sprang the most beautiful sight I have ever seen: a cop.

Blocking my path, he said, "Just a minute, bud, where do you think you're running to?"

I skidded to a stop, panting. "I'm being chased by a couple of guys. I think they're out to mug me," I said, out of breath.

He moved in, frisking me before I could explain, and in seconds had my Smith & Wesson and was looking very annoyed about it. And of course, my two assailants were now nowhere to be seen. They would have seen the squad car before I did.

It took a little while to get it all straightened out, with me mentioning Shunk's name at least four times and much careful reading of licenses and other documents in my possession. In the end they gave me back my property, including the Smith & Wesson. I explained about Spinoza McWilliams being involved in the case I was working on, and that the two Afro haircuts chasing me were his men, and that I didn't really think they were out to mug me, but more likely to kill me.

Chuckling, they gave me a lift over to Isabel's apartment. Very funny. If I had told them about hijacking the hundred thousand they might have understood about it not being so funny.

The ride was very uncomfortable. The squad car was one of those with a heavy metal grille between the front seat and the back, and no handles for opening the back doors on the inside. A prisoner, you get exposed to a lot of curious glances from passersby when the car pauses for a stop light or heavy traffic. One fat lady spat in my direction and said, "I hope they electrify you." I leered at her. "I'll be back for you, sweetie, when I get out," I said. She turned and waddled off as fast as she could go.

Isabel was looking very seductive in her short nightgown and short bathrobe. Kathy was looking very unseductive in virtually the same costume, only topped by a blank, meanish-looking face and a lot of plastic hair curlers. She doesn't like me either.

I explained the emergency to Isabel, and suggested that they let me bed down on the sofa. Isabel and Kathy had a mild argument about it.

"If they see men leaving here early in the

morning, they'll think we're like those girls next door," said Kathy. The building two doors down was known to house some plush cat parlors, and had been raided a couple of times.

"That's ridiculous," said Isabel. "We can't put him out with killers lurking in the dark."

"Killers!" sneered Kathy, flouncing off into the bedroom and closing the door with a hard click.

Isabel made coffee and scrambled me some eggs, and while I ate she fiddled around with my .38, pointing it and saying "Bang, bang." When I'm around her I remove all the shells and then put the safety on just to be absolutely sure. My job sort of fascinates her. She doesn't know whether to love it or hate it, and whether or not I'm some sort of an establishment lackey who shouldn't be approved of. Working with the police, who are misguided tools of the power structure, I am definitely suspect. On the other hand, she loves me. Or if she doesn't love me, she's one of the world's greatest actresses. The year we cop out in Spain or Italy, we'll figure it all out. As I keep telling her, at least it's not a boring job. Actually, it's getting a little too exciting.

We listened to some records, with the volume low, and fooled around a little, keeping in mind that you had to go through the living room to get to the bathroom, and that it would be just like Kathy to have to go at the most embarrassing possible time.

The sofa was not too comfortable, but I guess I was exhausted, because I slept soundly. I woke up at seven feeling great, and only vaguely worried about Spinoza McWilliams.

Isabel heard me knocking around in the kitchen, making coffee, and came in looking sleepy and very lovely.

"Call in sick," I said. "I have the day off."

"I can't call in sick," she said, "that wouldn't be fair."

She's a very honest girl. But how honest can you get?

"But I do have some vacation days coming to me," she said, "and we're not so busy. I could take one." She sat down and brushed some of her long, blond hair away from her right eye. Leave it alone, and she can only see out of one eye. "But what'll we do?"

I looked out the kitchen window. Even in the air shaft you could see the rain pouring down. What did one do on a bitter-cold, wet day in March? Other than the obvious, like staying in bed all day.

"Why don't we do something real weird, like, like going to Atlantic City?" I didn't want to go anywhere in New York, with the possibility of Spinoza or Abdul turning up. It was bad enough to have them after me, without involving Isabel.

"Atlantic City?"

"Why not? We can walk in the rain on the boardwalk, and have a great lobster dinner. It'll be deserted this time of year."

She poured herself a cup of coffee and we talked about other possibilities, like puttering around the Museum of Modern Art or the Metropolitan. We decided on Atlantic City.

We read the *Times,* ate breakfast, and drank several more cups of coffee until Kathy left for work, a smirk on her face. While I showered, Isabel went out and bought supplies for me. Toothbrush, razor, shaving lather, underwear, socks, and a shirt. The shirt was conservative, with purple, maroon, white, yellow, and black stripes.

I hadn't been to Atlantic City in years, and being new to the business world, if you can call my rather esoteric occupation a part of it, I didn't know that the city fathers had figured out how to keep Atlantic City busy even on cold, rainy days in March. There were two major conventions going on, and one massive trade show. The American Fretwork Manufacturers Association, the National Association of National Association Secretaries, and the National Institute of Non-Federally Insured Banks. The place was teeming with both rain and people, like New York at five in the afternoon.

I will say that Isabel has a sweet nature. The boardwalk was certainly deserted, but the rain was coming down in buckets and it wasn't really feasible to do the two-lovers-walking-in-the-rain-on-the-deserted-boardwalk bit. A drizzle, yes. Getting soaked to the skin is something else. So we wandered around Convention Hall looking at the Fretwork booths and collecting samples in shopping bags provided for the purpose.

We did manage the big lobster dinner, but prior to it we had to wait in line an hour to get a table.

On the way back to New York in the bus Isabel maintained that it had been a very interesting day and she wasn't sorry we spent it in Atlantic City. I suppose it did prove we can enjoy each other even under adverse circumstances.

Sitting in the bus, with the rain dribbling down the window panes, New York drew steadily closer, and I had to start thinking about Spinoza. I couldn't go on being a fugitive from Afro haircuts for the rest of my life. Dammit, Barnes or Shunk would have to do something to take the heat off. They owed it to me. In the meantime, what about my immediate future? I couldn't camp at Isabel's indefinitely. I was afraid to go to my apartment, even in broad daylight. Abdul might well be waiting for me inside the place, sitting right in my living room. Of course, Shunk could send a couple of cops with me, and I could at least collect some clothes. Maybe I should go to Europe for two or three months? Anything I could think of was expensive, impractical, and a damned nuisance.

At the apartment, Isabel and Kathy had another argument about my sleeping over again, and Isabel won, being definitely the stronger personality.

I telephoned Barnes and complained bitterly about the situation. He agreed that it was a bad scene. He said meet him at Consolidated in the morning and he would demand that Shunk provide me some sort of protection. Protective custody was probably what he would offer, the skunk.

"Consolidated? I thought we were fired from there." I asked.

"We are. Dick Wallace of National Group asked for the meeting to brief him on a couple of points. Shunk will be there."

Kathy, who had been eavesdropping, decided I really was in danger. She told Isabel I could stay as long as I liked, and she wouldn't complain, even though it was a nuisance, having a strange man around the place.

7

The long gray Cadillac limousine was empty, I thought. It was parked about twenty-five feet from Consolidated's entrance and even though I was still being very cautious, it didn't seem likely that they would come after me in daylight, right on the doorstep of the police station, figuratively speaking. Feeling relatively safe, I was still nervous enough to be clutching the butt of my .38 as I walked past. Something hit me between the shoulder blades, hard. I yanked the Smith & Wesson out and wheeled in time to see a rack about two inches in diameter bouncing on the pavement. The next few seconds were confused. About four people poured out of the Cadillac—Abdul, Cyril, and two blacks I hadn't seen before. One of them hit me in the knees with a tackle as professional as any you see at Shea Stadium. I went down shooting, but unfortunately didn't hit anybody. The others piled on. In the melee, a hard black fist clouted me in the jaw. Somebody else grabbed my shoulders and lifting me, banged my head hard on the pavement. I was stepped on repeatedly. "Help!" is a very inadequate word, but I yelled it a few times, as loud as I could.

In less than a minute they had carried me, still struggling and yelling, to the Cadillac and thrown me in the back. They had evidently been waiting awhile, because their parking space had shrunk and was now too tight to wheel out of fast. In reverse, the driver gunned the motor and slammed into the car behind hard enough to knock it back a yard. Still thrashing around, I saw Doris Preeble's startled face in the doorway of her apartment building.

"Preeble!" I yelled. "Police!"

That's the last thing I remember.

When I came to, it was because my eyelid was hurting. Abdul was peeling it back to see whether I was really unconscious. I looked around slowly, feeling pains just about everywhere you can feel pain. My ankles were handcuffed to the legs of a chair, and my wrists were handcuffed together, my arms strained around the back of the chair. Very awkward and uncomfortable. I guessed we were in a basement room. The floor was damp concrete, and the walls were stained plasterboard. There were no windows.

"You ain't such a smartass now, are you, Harvey Motherbanger?"

I nodded. Why argue?

"Man, you cause us more trouble than six redneck sheriffs."

I shook my head. Some loose parts of my brain hurt, rattling around.

"What did I ever do to you?" I asked. As if I didn't know.

"*You* know what you did."

The door opened and Spinoza came in, looking as dapper as ever.

"You didn't kill my old friend? That, man, is *my* pleasure."

"No, he still breathing."

I was, but very quietly.

Spinoza came over and slapped me hard. "You lousy son of a bitch, what you mean, stealing my money?"

After the waves of pain and noise died down I said, "It was robbery money. It was my job to get that money back." I wasn't in a very strong position. My excuse was about as good as that of an ex-Nazi guard testifying in Tel Aviv.

Spinoza snorted. "That wasn't no robbery money. That cash belonged to some of the meanest cats in this town. I had to pay every penny of it back out of my own bank account."

I shrugged. Even that hurt. "What can I say? I'm sorry."

"You sorry."

"I'm *sorry*."

He slapped me again. If my brains got much

more scrambled, I wouldn't be much use to Isabel. I let my chin sag onto my chest and pretended to fade out.

I got a bucket of water in my face, but it felt good.

"I'm going to take that hundred thousand right out of your hide. My pound of flesh, man."

I waited, my eyes open.

"I'm going to send a little piece of you to Consolidated every day until they give me back my cash. I think tomorrow we send them an ear.

"Lieutenant Shunk has it. He'll never give it up."

"Man, you just better hope he do."

Spinoza wheeled around and marched out of the room.

Abdul said, "I'm going to leave you here awhile, man, but you make any noise I'm coming back and cut your tongue right out. You see this?" He pulled out a wicked-looking straight-edge razor and held it under my nose. "Put your tongue out, and I show you."

I kept my mouth closed.

When he moved away I said, "You can depend on it. I'm going to be very quiet."

He grinned and went to the door. I heard it open, then the snick of a bolt being shot on the outside.

There was nothing in the room but an old Army cot and another chair. The only light came from a single bulb suspended in the center of the

184

room, about sixty watts' worth, I estimated. My arms were pulled so tightly against the sides of the back of the chair that they gave me continuous pain where the wood cut into the muscles.

It was an understatement to say that I was depressed. I've never felt so low. Panic, too, if you can imagine the combination. Were they really going to cut me up? Would you put it past Spinoza, high on smack?

I tried to ease my arms up by making an effort to stand. I was shackled to tightly. All I succeeded in doing was rocking the chair, almost falling backward, which would have given me another nice crack on the skull. I tried to lean forward and stand, but that didn't work either. I almost fell flat on my face.

There was nothing to do but sit, a dull mass of aches and pains, and wait. It was hard to estimate time. I spent some of it reviewing my past. It wasn't flashing before me as it is supposed to with a drowning man, but unreeling painfully, depressingly slowly. Finally I drifted into a numb state, thinking of nothing.

Abdul returned with a large, new plastic bucket. In it was a paper bag. He removed the bag and set it on the cot. Then he put the bucket over in a far corner of the room.

"Do you want to relieve yourself, man?" he asked.

I nodded.

He took a key ring from the pocket of his tight

jeans. "I'm going to unlock you. Don't try nothing, man. Dig? I cut you to shreds."

He unlocked the handcuffs. First my wrists, then my feet.

I tried to stand, and almost toppled over. It felt like a number of pieces of broken glass had been imbedded through my body, and were being rotated with my movement.

I groaned, swaying. Abdul caught my arm to steady me.

"I'm a sick man," I said. "I wouldn't be surprised if I'm dying."

Abdul said, "You feel better when you have some coffee."

I staggered over to the bucket and made use of it.

When I turned around I saw that Abdul had opened the paper bag and removed the contents, a container of coffee and two hamburgers. Waves of pain were still rolling through me as I staggered over to the cot, which I could hardly see, my eyes were so bleary. He handed me the container of coffee and I took a couple of sips blindly. There was something solid and squirmy in my mouth. I spat quickly.

A cockroach hit the concrete floor, shook himself, and scurried off. "Jeez! A cockroach in my coffee." Abdul watched it make for a crack in the wall. "What you complaining about, man? At least you got a *fresh* cockroach. He still alive."

I staggered over to the bucket and threw up.

"I think that's pretty rotten, putting a cockroach in my coffee," I said, gasping.

Abdul shrugged. "It wasn't intentional, man. In this kind of place, you get used to finding cockroaches in your food. Rat dung too."

I made it back to the cot and sat down, holding my head.

"My boss is a hypochondriac," I said. "I carry around a lot of medicines for him. Do you mind if I take some? I feel pretty sick." I was afraid to reach in my pockets. Abdul was so quick with that razor, and he might misunderstand.

Abdul scratched his chin. "I got no objection."

"I have to reach in my pockets."

"Go ahead. You got nothing in there that worries me."

I reached for Barnes's assortment of pills. "What happened to my .38?"

Abdul watched me unload various plastic containers and small bottles, which I lined up on the floor. "Who knows, man. On the pavement outside Consolidated, probably."

Pepto-Bismol, Donnatal, Bufferin, Gelusil, Excedrin, meprobamate, Seconal, placebos, codeine, Anacin, Compoz. Codeine was definitely called for. I took a pill out of the small container and chewed it up.

"Man, you sure got some medicine chest there."

I swallowed the bitter-tasting codeine. "Yeah."

"Man, you got anything that collection for sinus? I got a sinus that's giving me hell."

I stared at Abdul. My eyes were beginning to focus a little better. Too bad I didn't have something I could feed him that would be a real mickey. The Seconal might make him sleepy, but he was probably sophisticated enough to know what a red sleeping-drug capsule looked like. The meprobamate was a tranquilizer, and Abdul was tranquil enough.

"You try aspirin or Bufferin?"

"Don't seem to help."

"How about Seconal?"

"Sleeping pills?"

"A lot of people take them for sinus." That was a lie, but what could I say?

"I never heard that."

"Maybe codeine, the stuff I just took? It's a general pain killer. But it's a habit-forming, morphine-derived drug, I think." I handed him the container.

Abdul stared at the label curiously. "I don't dig drugs," he said, "but I'll try one. My sinus is killing me." He took one of the small pills and handed the container back. I scooped the other containers up and distributed them in various pockets.

"Do you mind if I stretch out on the cot?"

"Be my guest."

I pushed the bag of hamburgers aside and lay

down. The codeine would work eventually, and would help some.

"I'm going to put the cuffs back on you."

I nodded. There didn't seem to be any point in arguing.

The codeine began to take effect. I felt vaguely better and drifted off to sleep.

Some time later Abdul came back, accompanied by Spinoza, who was holding a telephone, a jack plug on the end of its loose cord. He bent over and plugged it into the wall.

"They tell me a call can't possibly be traced with this kind of setup," he said, straightening up. "This telephone don't even belong to the Telephone Company, and this wire is spliced into a line four buildings away." He looked at me hard, his lips turned way down. "But we ain't taking chances, whitey. You don't talk long. I'm going to give you maybe ten words to tell about your misery."

He dialed and waited. "Hello, Barnes? Hold on." He held the handset up to my face. I heard Barnes say, "Larry?"

"Yeah," I said. "Send the money. They're going to cut me up."

"Larry, we can't—"

Spinoza broke the connection. Great. We can't. Was the money impounded? It would probably take a judge or an act of Congress to get it away from the district attorney's office. It was evidence, and it was a lot of other legal-beagle red tape. Even if if wasn't robbery money, it was illegal money. Otherwise the rightful owner could simply come forward and claim it.

"How do they even know where to send it?" I asked.

"They know. We in touch. This phone call just to let them know you're still *alive*."

I turned my face to the wall.

"They got until noon tomorrow to return my hundred thousand. If they don't, we start sending you back to them, piece by piece," said Spinoza. He gave me a light kick. "And *that* will be my very great pleasure. All Gaul is divided into three parts. We will divide you into a great number of little parts. Man, you going to be the bloodiest subdivision in history."

I heard the door open and close. It was Spinoza leaving, because I heard Abdul say, "Man, that pill you gave me was all right. My front sinuses don't ache no more. What you say it was?"

"Codeine. Don't take it too often, it's very habit-forming."

"You got to have a prescription?"

"Yeah."

"I'll have to get me a prescription."

Spinoza was going to subdivide me. Larry Howe Estates. It was a lousy thing to think about. I wished Abdul would go away and let me get back to sleep. The codeine had really taken hold. I drifted off.

During the night I woke up because some rats were making love under the cot. How do I know they were making love? A Navy ratologist told me. I was on Okinawa for a while, en route to Vietnam, and they used to get under the floorboards of the tent and make the same kind of noises. Shrill yipping, squealing, and other unearthly sounds. The Navy ratologist would come and put poison around. The rats were supposed to eat the poison, head for the nearest water, a stream about fifty feet from our bivouac area, drink, and die right on the spot. It didn't work that way. They always managed to get back and die under the floorboards of the tent.

Some of my pains were severe again. Fortunately Abdul had handcuffed my wrists in front of me. With some difficulty I managed to get into my jacket pocket and find the codeine container. Opening it, I took another pill, and lay back vaguely worried about the rats. Would they, finally surfeited and bored with lovemaking, decide to come up and chew on me? I was no helpless baby with milk on my cheeks. In fact, I hadn't eaten since yesterday morning. I remembered the bag of hamburgers. Groping around awkwardly I found it and threw it as far as I could from the cot, two-handed. Then I went back to sleep with my hands cupped over my face.

It must have been morning. It was hard to tell. Abdul came in with a white paper bag. Coffee and hamburgers. I was feeling better, and hungry.

"This is good coffee, man. No roaches. I went all the way to Chock Full o'Nuts for it."

I sat up and he unlocked my wrists. The condemned man ate a hearty breakfast. "I appreciate your getting me coffee without roaches in it," I said, munching.

He tossed his Afro contemptuously. "Black people don't like roaches any more than you do."

The onions in the hamburgers were giving me indigestion. Wasn't I in enough trouble without being castigated for the sins of my forefathers?

"You can't fight any black-white war with me. Spinoza knows I've always tried to help get justice for blacks."

"Yeah."

He relocked the handcuffs on my wrists and left, locking the door loudly. I sat on the cot and stared into space. Across the room were hamburger wrappings from the night before. The rats hadn't left a crumb. If Spinoza cut off my ear, it would be very painful. Assuming I survived, how much would a new ear cost? Cosmetic surgery came high. Barnes would undoubtedly feel obligated to stake me for it. Could it be possible that Spinoza would really cut off my ear? I was afraid he would. He was insane, or verging on insanity. His big brain was out of gear. The duel. His anger was definitely psychopathic. He had reason to be angry now, but that afternoon he had no reason to be homicidally angry with me. Expressing concern about his being on heroin was not a mortal insult.

The pain in my head was now more bearable, and my other aches were not as persistent. I decided I could do without the codeine, and settled for two Bufferin. I chewed them up the way Barnes does, without water, and managed to find enough saliva to swallow them.

My watch was broken. It had stopped at eight fifty-two yesterday morning. What time was it? How near noon was it? My heart started to pound, and waves of dizziness swept over me.

I got up and hopped across the room to the bucket, only falling down once in the process. After using the bucket, I hopped to the door, twisted the knob, and pulled. Locked solidly and tightly. With some difficulty, I braced my feet against the jamb and, leaning sideways, pulled the knob with all my might. I hoped the leverage of my weight and muscles might snap the old lock. Futile hope. All it did was groan and creak a little, and my hands were bruised and hurt from the effort.

If I were only one of these superman foreign agents. I would then cleverly unlock the handcuffs with a pick previously concealed in my left nostril. Help would be forthcoming from a transmitter concealed in the lining of my shorts. Abdul would be dead, because I would have handed him my cyanide pill in place of the codeine. Also I would have a tiny gun that shot poison needles carefully hidden in my right cheek. When Spinoza returned, I would tongue the little gun into position, open my lips slightly, and *zap!* Spinoza would go down, clutching his throat. Cyril would get it too, *zap!*

I resolved that if I got out alive, I would study up on being a foreign agent. I felt extremely foolish, hopping around the room like a damned bunny rabbit. Conceivably I could pick up a chair and clobber the next guy who came into the room. But if there was more than one, the second one would have a field day with his razor. I tried lifting one of the chairs, grasping the back. With my hands cuffed together, I couldn't get a good grip on it. Holding it by the center ribs I managed to lift it over my head. One of them cracked from the pressure, and I had to lower it. I had a feeling that smacking Abdul with it would only annoy him. He was taller than me, and the arc would not be large enough to get much steam behind it. I hefted the other one. The center ribs creaked. They were spindly, and only about three eighths of an inch in diameter.

I could smash one of the chairs by banging it on the concrete floor and perhaps tear loose one of the legs as a weapon. The noise might bring Abdul running. But I couldn't think of anything else. I lifted the chair over my head and swung it down crashing to the floor as hard as I could. Nothing broke but the center ribs, leaving jagged pieces which could have sliced open my wrist arteries but didn't. It made a lot of noise. I quickly picked it up and threw it down hard. More noise. One of the legs cracked, but not enough to break it away from the seat. I lifted it and threw it down again.

The door lock snicked and Abdul and Cyril rushed in. I picked up the chair and tried to hop backward, holding it in front of me. I'm not used to backward hopping, and managed to sit down rather painfully

"What the hell you trying to do, man?" yelled Abdul.

He snatched the chair away. Then the two of them grabbed me and threw me on the cot. Abdul sat on me while Cyril went for some rope.

"You don't have to sit on me. I know when I'm licked."

"You shut up, man."

Cyril came back, and in about three minutes they had me tied down so tightly I could hardly move. I could lift my head a little and look around a bit, and that was about it.

"Now you won't be busting up no more furniture."

"What would *you* do if you were in my position?" I asked.

"I'd sweat."

"How's your sinus?" Androcles took a thorn out of the lion's paw, and the lion was grateful later. He refused to eat Androcles.

"You shut up," said Abdul. Couldn't have cared less about the great pill I gave him.

Spinoza came in. He stood over me. "I have reviewed your horoscope, and the signs are all bad. You are most definitely in a poor phase of the moon. And you even in trouble with the sun, man, because it is now *high noon*, and your good friends have not responded to my request for the return of my *money*. "

I crooked my neck, trying to see him. He was standing there with his chest stuck out like a penguin.

"My *money*," he repeated.

"I'm in favor of their returning it. You heard me tell Barnes, *send the money*. What else can I do?"

"*Ich weiss nicht was sol es bedeuten, das ich so traurig bin*," said Spinoza. Now he was quoting Heine at me. He didn't know why he was so sad. Was he sad because he didn't have his money back, or was he sad because he was going to cut me up?

"Cheer up," I said, "they'll probably have the money over first thing tomorrow."

"I am suddenly overcome with *Weltschmerz*."

"You're remembering the good old days when we were *close friends*," I said, hopefully.

Spinoza grunted contemptuously. "I am

thinking of the good old days when there was no complications over the hundred thousand. Fifteen percent of which was to be mine."

"Why would a rich man like you care about a lousy fifteen thousand?'

"It is now a lousy hundred thousand."

"Why do you care about a lousy hundred thousand?"

He sniffed hard. I could see his nostrils distending. "I have a passionate concern about every dollar that is due me. People who owe me money and don't pay suddenly find themselves crippled. Permanently. Sometimes they find a home in a box, six feet under."

My neck was hurting from the strain of twisting it upward to look at him. "Great philosophers seldom care about material wealth. You are a great philosopher. Money couldn't buy the brilliance of your reasoning. You have great thoughts, great propositions to unfold. You should be writing them down, not concerning yourself with material things like money." It was a long speech, and futile, I was sure. I let my head fall back.

He chuckled. "White boy speak with forked tongue. Try to screw simple black man with words dripping honey."

"You black son of a bitch," I muttered into the air, "you're about as simple as a computer gone haywire."

"Nevertheless." He let it hang for a moment.

"We must send your friends a token of your affection. A token of your nonaffection, to be more accurate. It may stimulate them to act faster, with a treasured piece of you to contemplate."

"Don't do it. It's not worth it."

Over in Cyril's direction I heard a *snick, snick, snick* sound. I twisted my neck and craned to see. He was honing his big, straight-edge razor.

"How about I cut off his ear?"

"In Islam," said Abdul, "with a thief, they chop off his hand. The hand that steals will steal no more."

"I'm not a thief," I yelled. "I took the money because I thought it had been stolen from my employer. *Loyalty,* not thievery."

There was a silence.

"How's that for *loyalty*?" I asked hopefully.

"He loyal," said Cyril, chuckling.

"*Pereunt et imputantur.* We shall not cut off his ear. One day we finish our duel. With sabers. The ears will be mine for slicing," said Spinoza.

"Thanks. I'll be looking forward to it." I stared at the ceiling, perspiration trickling off my forehead.

"I think we chop off a finger. Pinky. Left hand."

"You're saving my sword hand for our duel."

"Go get your little hatchet, Cyril."

"There'll be a lack of balance," I said wildly. "You know how important the left hand is for balance." I twisted my neck to look at Spinoza. "I can't duel with a missing finger on my left hand."

Spinoza looked annoyed. "Man, you really full of shit today. That little finger ain't going to affect your balance."

"Of course it will. Ask anybody."

He shrugged. "Maybe I got to sacrifice one of my ears for slicing."

"Why don't we just make another strong telephone call? I'll scream just as loud as if you were really cutting off my ear."

"You going to scream when I cut off your ear?" asked Cyril.

"You're damned right. For a month straight."

Spinoza snapped his fingers. "Got it! We'll send them a pint of your blood. A pint a day until they return my money."

My perspiration was turning to cold chills. "That has to be done by an expert. I could bleed to death!"

Spinoza paced up and down for a moment. "Cyril here, he's a graduate undertaker. He not only knows how to take out your blood, when it's all gone he fill you up with embalming fluid."

I stared at the ceiling some more. It was stained where a pipe leaked. What could I say?

"Cyril, you hop over to the funeral parlor and get your equipment."

"Okay, Spin. You wait right there, Harvey, hear?"

How many pints of blood did a guy have? One

199

didn't bother me. I had given to the blood bank several times. It was better than having an ear or a finger cut off, but still very repulsive having it done by a graduate undertaker. How did I ever get mixed up with this bunch of madmen? All over a lousy little embezzlement in a crummy little bodega. I hoped Madam Perez developed galloping hives for the rest of her life.

Cyril came back with some tubing, a hollow needle, and an empty pint of old Grand-Dad.

"Make a fist. I got to find your vein."

I reluctantly made a fist. Better he should find the vein than an artery.

He found it, expertly, and my life's blood began to drain away into the bottle of Old Grand-Dad.

At the blood bank, how often did they allow donors to give or sell a pint? It seemed to me it was ten days or two weeks. How dangerous was it to lose a second pint in twenty-four hours?

I began to burn with an unreasoning rage. When I got loose, I would track down Spinoza, Cyril, and Abdul and kill them all. With hollow bullets. The kind that spread in the body and blow a hole a foot in diameter when they come out. They would die in agony, one by one. I would step on Spinoza's smug face while he lay dying, and grind my heel slowly. I would exterminate them like roaches.

Cyril removed the needle, wiped my arm with alcohol, left the wad of cotton, and roughly doubled my wrist back to hold the cotton in place. "Keep it there for five minutes," he said.

He capped the bottle of Old Grand-Dad and held it up for me to see. "Want a swig?"

My stomach turned over several times and I thought I was going to throw up.

How much blood did the human body have? I seemed to remember it was five liters. The adult male body contains about five liters. How much was a liter? Was it about a pint, or about a quart? Damn these European measurements. And why in the hell weren't we on the metric system anyway? How stupid can you be? Inches, yards, miles. Even miles were measured in tenths.

A liter was more than a quart. No, it was less than a pint. I couldn't remember.

I would dedicate the rest of my life to killing Spinoza. We'd duel with sabers all right. Except that he wouldn't have any saber. I would chop him to pieces, slowly. I'd leave his legs until the last, so he could keep backing around the room the way I had to.

Did I have five pints, or ten pints?

Kill, kill, kill. It gave me some comfort to keep repeating the word to myself. Spinoza, you're already a dead man, you just don't know it.

It was probably late in the afternoon when Spinoza came back with the telephone. He plugged it in and dialed, repeating the same procedure. When Barnes got on, Spinoza held the handset close to me.

"Larry, for God's sake, is that really your *blood*?"

"You're damned right it is. SEND THAT MONEY! They're bleeding me to death! SEND THE MONEY!"

"Larry, we're trying—"

Spinoza broke the connection.

They were trying. Great. Why didn't he say, "We're *sending*"?

"He trying," said Abdul.

"He better *send*," said Spinoza.

They went away and I lay there brooding. I occupied myself thinking of other great ways to kill them. After a while I got a little sick. I'm essentially a nonviolent type, and I hate to even step on a roach.

Abdul came back with a large paper bag. Coffee and three hamburgers, very rare.

"You need to get your strength back, losing all that blood."

I drank the coffee and ate the hamburgers without comment. Why try to talk to madmen? Doomed madmen at that. Nonviolent as I was, I would surely kill them.

Spinoza came, and stalked around the room looking important.

"You mad, aren't you?" he asked.

That was the understatement of the century. I think up until they actually took a pint of my blood that I really didn't believe they were going to mutilate me, that Spinoza was talking big to scare the bejesus out of me, which he did. Now that I knew they weren't fooling, I was strangely no longer afraid. My only emotion was cold rage.

"I said, you mad, aren't you?"

"I've nothing to say to you, Spinoza."

"*Sic eunt fata hominum.*"

"My Latin's rusty," I said coldly.

"It was necessary to spill your blood."

"Yeah."

"Tomorrow we send them two pints. One from me, and one from Abdul."

I looked up at him. He really was cracked.

"They've got to understand that this is a desperate situation. Desperate for me as well as for you."

"Why?"

"I told you that money belonged to some of the meanest cats in town. Day after tomorrow is *my* deadline." He sliced his forefinger across his throat.

"You said you paid them back out of your own money."

"I didn't. I don't have that kind of liquid cash. I offered to sign over three of my buildings, but these cats aren't in a position to own buildings. They want that hundred thousand. In tens. Nothing else."

"Couldn't you sell the buildings to somebody else?"

He laughed. "You kidding? Who wants these old rat holes? Even *giving* them away, I doubt if I could raise seventy thousand dollars on all three."

So Spinoza's life was in danger. I felt a little better about the crazy situation. At least he wasn't insane. Or was he? Our afternoon duel wasn't the work of a sane man.

"If it wasn't robbery money, what the hell was it? It had some connection with Gates, because you got the damned locker key from him."

"You shut up. It's none of your business. You interfered enough already," said Spinoza. "And you keep talking to me in that tone of voice, we take two pints from *you* tomorrow."

I decided I'd better shut up.

Later in the evening Abdul brought me three more hamburgers and another carton of coffee. I swallowed two Seconal capsules with the last of the coffee. It was hard to face another night with the rats. I conked out, but not completely. I could hear them shrieking and squealing and scurrying around bumping into things. Drugged, I covered my face with the palms of my hands and slept on.

The Seconal hit me so hard I slept right up to high noon.

Spinoza came in looking grim, followed by Abdul and Cyril.

"*Le jeu ne vaut pas la chandelle,*" said Spinoza. "I resent having to give a pint of my blood."

"No money?"

"None.'

204

"Remember, Barnes said they were *trying*." I was in a panic. It was too soon for me to lose another pint. It might injure me seriously. "The money might come any minute."

Cyril was carrying two pint bottles, one an empty Johnny Walker Red, and the other Olde Bourbon.

Spinoza rolled up his sleeve. "Cyril, take a pint of my blood," he said, "and be goddamned careful about how you do it. You give me hepatitis or something and I'll cut you to ribbons."

Cyril filled the Johnny Walker bottle with Spinoza's blood. I got a crick in my neck watching.

"Abdul says he can't give a pint. It's against his religion to give blood," said Spinoza, holding his forearm bent tightly to hold the cotton wadding.

Perspiration popped out on my forehead. Another pint from me so soon might kill me, for all I knew. If the body only had *five* pints. If a liter was a pint. Or was it a quart? My heart started to pound.

"You don't need more than a pint. They'll be frantic when they get it. Anyway, the money may come any minute!"

"It can't come any minute. The time for picking it up is past."

"One pint's enough!"

"I can't take a chance. If I don't get that money tonight, it's going to be very bad news for Spinoza."

"With two pints, they'll think I'm already dead. Three pints in two days!"

Spinoza shook his head. "I got to scare the shit out of them. I got to get *action*." He turned to Cyril. "How about you give a pint, Cyril?"

Cyril said, "Uh, uh. I got a date tonight. I need all my strength."

Spinoza did some pacing. "Tell you what. Cyril you give a half pint, and Larry give a half pint. We kill him, we'll be in as much trouble with the law as we are over the goddamned hundred thousand."

Cyril said, "Uh, uh. Let Abdul give half."

Abdul said, "Uh, uh. It's against my religion."

"You lying. It ain't against your religion."

"It's an insult to my body, which I keep clean. Unlike some other characters I could mention, who eat pig flesh and are not clean."

"What you mean, man, I take a bath every day."

"You eat pig flesh."

"You mean ham and bacon? Man, you out of your mind."

"Now listen," Spinoza yelled. "Quiet!" He turned to Cyril. "Cyril, I'm asking your cooperation. And I expect to get it."

Cyril was very unhappy. "You mean I got to give eight ounces of my good blood for this lousy Harvey Motherbanger? I got better use for my blood."

"I'm *asking* your cooperation."

"Besides, I can't stick myself. I just can't."

"I'll stick you," I said quickly. "I was an Army medic. I know just how to do it." That was a lie, but I needed that eight ounces.

Cyril sterilized the needle with alcohol, then rolled up his sleeve, grumbling. "You better find that vein the first stick, man. I ain't going to have you messing up my arm, sticking me a half dozen times." He doubled up his fist and stood by the cot, making a vein. I got it on the second try, with a lot of complaining about my missing the first time.

I watched the Olde Bourbon bottle slowly fill. From my angle, tied to the cot, I couldn't see whether it was half full or not.

"Hey, man, that's more than half full."

"How do you cut it off?"

He removed the needle himself, grabbed a wad of cotton and held it tightly against the wound.

I was definitely an ounce or two ahead. It only took six or seven from me to fill the bottle.

"The message with this package will be, 'Tomorrow we send three more pints, and we start filling him up with embalming fluid.' If that don't get the hundred thousand, we in big trouble," said Spinoza.

I was beginning to feel weak and dizzy. It was probably dangerous to give even six or seven more ounces. I sank back and groaned.

"You feel bad?" asked Spinoza.

"Rotten."

"You going to feel worse if they don't give me back my money."

He left, carrying the two bottles carefully.

I went back to sleep. The Seconal had been a strong dose. I had never taken more than one at a time before.

When I woke up, Spinoza was back for the telephone routine.

"Larry, Larry! Is that really your blood?" Barnes yelled.

"Yes,' I whispered, "send the money. I'm very weak. They're bleeding me to death. I don't have long. I need a transfusion." I gasped it out, whispering the whole message.

"The money—" Spinoza cut the connection.

"Now why did you do that? We still don't know whether they're going to pay," I asked, irritated.

"They'll pay," said Spinoza. "My intuition tells me. That deathbed speech of yours was okay. But it took a little too long. All that whispering and gasping. Shunk's been tearing this town apart looking for me. I ain't taking any more chances."

He walked out, slamming the door. Cyril gathered up his equipment and followed. I suppose he had to take the stuff back to the funeral parlor.

Abdul sat watching me. I watched the ceiling. If the money still didn't arrive, what then? Spinoza hadn't wanted to kill me, but if he was going to be wiped out himself, he might decide to take me along for companionship. Also, there was the matter of what I could do to him once released. Kidnapping is a pretty serious offense. On the other hand, I reasoned hopefully, if he meant to kill me, he wouldn't have worried about taking too much blood. Maybe he was afraid I might pass out, go into a coma, be unable to talk to Barnes. If they thought I was dead, they'd never give up the money.

"Abdul, you hungry?"

"No, man."

"I was thinking if you were hungry, maybe you might get us some hamburgers and coffee."

"I can't leave at this time."

I continued to stare at the ceiling, becoming hypnotized by the shapes of the cracks and stains, and little dark things that seemed to move, but you couldn't be sure.

Spinoza finally came back. He marched into the room and closed the door briskly.

"Well, man, I think maybe we out of trouble. If we are, we won't be seeing each other again for a *long* time. What I mean is, it *better* be a long time."

I lifted my head and twisted my neck to see him.

"Should you indicate a willingness to the police to testify against me, Abdul, or Cyril, we'll be seeing each other sooner than would be healthy for you." He clasped his hands behind his back and puffed out his chest. "You brought this situation on yourself by stealing our money. By doing this you have not only endangered my life, my future financial prospects, but have also made me a nervous wreck. Be thankful that I have written it off as stupidity on your part, not malice."

"I'm grateful," I said, trying to keep the irony out of my tone.

It wouldn't do me much good to promise not to testify against him. It would be meaningless. There would be a lot of pressure on me from Shunk, too.

"Your line, my friend, is that you were kidnaped by a bunch of Afros you never saw before in your life. Everybody knows us niggers all look alike to white people, so nobody will be surprised when you study the police photo files for hours and find that you just can't be sure about anybody. Right?"

I nodded weakly.

"The reason you going to do this is not because you love your old buddy Spinoza, but because if you don't my people going to kill you. And that, my friend, is a promise about which I am deadly serious. They hold me for trial, you'll never live to testify."

"So I won't testify," I said, pretending to be more frightened than I was. "They're going to suspect you. They know where I got the hundred thousand. I can't help that.'

Spinoza snapped his fingers. "Man, they suspect me of a lot of things. They can't prove nothing without your testimony."

"Okay," I said. "I don't want to spend the rest of my life running away from Afro haircuts."

Spinoza's mouth twisted into a wry smile. "Besides, you know you *wrong*, stealing my money."

There he had it. I had been mulling around the rights and wrongs of it, and with my own peculiar set of moral standards, I had half sorted it out, as they say on Carnaby Street. If the money I took from Spinoza wasn't part of the Consolidated robbery loot, then I sort of had the kidnaping coming to me. Or worse. This being the case, I would not take part in prosecuting Spinoza. On the other hand, if it was part of the robbery money, I would be inclined to say to hell with his threats.

After Spinoza left, Abdul untied me. I sat up, stretching gratefully. As well as you can stretch with your hands cuffed.

"I'm going to leave you, man, with the door unlocked. And I don't want you to move out of this room for ten minutes."

"Hey, how about taking the handcuffs off?"

He grinned. "Man, you want everything the easy way." He went to the door. "Keep in mind what Spinoza said."

Ever try to hop up steps with your feet tied together? Don't. Even holding the rail with both hands, I stumbled and fell three times. The first-floor hall was obviously that of an abandoned

211

tenement. I hopped painfully to the boarded-up front door, which was unlocked, the hinges hanging loosely. Outside I had seven perilous steps to hop down.

Buildings all around seemed to be empty. The street was deserted. I hopped to the nearest corner, then headed in the direction of what looked like a major business street. It was hard work. A couple of middle-aged and rather fat black women came along, looking at me curiously.

"Where can I find the nearest cop?" I asked, puffing.

The one nearest me shook her head, and they hurried by. What would whitey be up to next?

I finally made it to the corner. Pitkin Avenue. I was in Brownsville. Miles from Harlem.

I hopped to the door of a liquor store, and managed to get it open and hop in. The proprietor drew a pistol and leveled it at me.

"Don't shoot! Get the cops! I've been kidnaped."

I sat on the floor and panted.

Barnes arrived with an ambulance in about seven minutes. I've never seen him so distraught.

"Give this man *blood!*" he yelled. "Immediately!"

He bent over me. "Larry! Thank God you're alive!" Then he turned back to the attendants. "*Blood,* give him *blood!*"

One of the attendants said, "We'll have to wait

until we get him to the hospital, doc," They lifted me on to the stretcher. "Upsa daisy, that's it."

Barnes fussed around, wild-eyed. "Careful there. Dammit, be careful with him!"

He sat in the back of the ambulance with me. "Don't talk. Conserve your strength," he said, digging for his cigarettes frantically. Those three pints of blood had really shaken him. I guess they would have shaken me.

We started off, the siren screaming. "How much is a liter?" I asked.

"What?" Barnes was lighting a cigarette, his hand shaking.

"Is a liter about a pint, or about a quart?"

"It's a little more than a quart. Why?"

"It's been bothering me."

"Don't talk. Wait until you get some blood."

8

The hospital whisked me into a routine of X-rays, blood-lettings, and other tests.

The doctor had long hair down to his shoulders, which I dig. I like to see a fellow freak doing something useful.

He was puzzled. "How much blood did you actually lose?"

"Confidential? Doctor-patient?"

"Okay."

"About twenty-three ounces."

"They said three pints."

"The others contributed the other pint and a half."

"The others?"

"The guys who kidnaped me."

He stared at me a long time. Probably thought I was kidding. Finally he said, "You're in pretty good shape. No bones broken, blood pressure okay. Some awfully bad bruises. No internal injuries or concussion, as far as I can tell. You'll find the going pretty stiff and painful for a while." He scratched his head. "You certain about the blood? That you only lost a pint and a half?"

215

I nodded.

"I think we'll give you a little plasma, just to be on the safe side."

After they finished giving me plasma, they let Barnes and Shunk come in. Isabel, I discovered later, was also waiting, but Shunk pulled his rank. It wasn't that I was too sick for more than two people; outsiders can't be present at a police interrogation.

Shunk said, "I always knew you were full of something, but I never suspected, ha, ha, that it was blood."

"Very funny," said Barnes.

"One thing that has been bugging me," I said quickly. "What is Gates's explanation of his meeting with Spinoza?"

Shunk shrugged. "Claims he was trying to make a deal on the Perez embezzlement."

"Do you believe that?"

"No."

"Do you think the stuff I hijacked was part of the robbery money?"

"I'm here to ask *you* questions." He smiled. "But just between the three of us, and unofficially, I don't think so. I also have an idea about where the money came from, but since I can't prove it, I'm not going to go spouting off about it."

Barnes asked, "How are you feeling?"

"Okay. They say I can get out tomorrow morning."

"Wonderful!"

Shunk frowned, as though to say, "Enough of this time-wasting sentimentality," and began barking questions at me. We finally established that while Spinoza was probably behind the kidnaping, I couldn't tie him to it through the people I saw. I described them in accurate detail as black, with Afro haircuts, of medium height and build, with shades ranging from very black to light chocolate. One had a star-shaped scar on his left forearm, another had a very flat nose and very thick lips, and the third, who had a thin nose, had pimples on his upper lip.

I could see endless line-ups ahead of me, but what could I do? Fortunately, I have an excellent memory.

"Did the doctor say you'd be strong enough to go back to work tomorrow? Or maybe you'd better rest a few days?" asked Barnes.

"Oh, I'm okay."

"I'm just wondering whether to keep Harry Weiner on."

"You working on the Long Island thing?"

Barnes's eyebrows lifted. "That's right, you need some bringing up to date. We're back on the Consolidated robbery. Wickersham of England decided that they wanted their own investigation."

"The insurance company?"

Barnes nodded.

"Makes sense," I said. "It being an inside job."

Barnes nodded again. "I'm very pleased. I resented being cut off right in the middle of things."

"Have you succeeded in identifying the guy Doris Preeble saw leaving Consolidated just before the police arrived?"

Shunk growled. "That dumb broad, she couldn't identify King Kong in a line-up with Sunday school kids."

"Her assumption that it was someone from Consolidated seems to be only that, just an assumption. Nothing that would stand up in court," said Barnes.

"Getting back to Spinoza's money," I said, "what took you so damned long?" I was still a little burned, and I had been waiting for an explanation to be volunteered.

Shunk went over and looked out the window. "The whole request was highly irregular," he said over his shoulder.

"Otto was certain his men would be able to pick up Spinoza in a matter of hours," said Barnes. "Then there were legal technicalities."

"In the meantime, I could have had my hand chopped off."

Barnes looked startled.

"I'm not kidding. That's what they were going to send you before they hit on the idea of the blood." Hand, finger, what's the difference?

Barnes stared at me gravely. "Without trying to excuse the delay, because it certainly had me

218

raving like a maniac, I'll have to admit that Otto here, and Hank Blomberg down in the district attorney's office, not only did everything they could, but actually stuck their respective necks out a mile to resolve it."

Shunk strolled back, grinning.

"While everyone was still arguing over legal technicalities, they simply requisitioned the *evidence* from the safe and delivered it to Spinoza's intermediary."

I was really touched.

"Theoretically, they could both go to jail," said Barnes.

"I'm touched," I said to Shunk.

"I would have done as much for a mangy little dog,"he said. Always gracious, Otto.

"Actually we tried to deliver the money the day before you got away. The intermediary never picked it up. Probably thought the police were watching," said Barnes.

"Were they?"

"Not from any place those sons of bitches could have known about," said Shunk.

They finally left and let Isabel come up. She was a little weepy and nervous, but had a bunch of my press clippings. As kidnapee, I had become famous overnight. The only pictures they had been able to locate were from my high school annual and a later one from my freak days, when I had shoulder-length hair and a huge black mustache. As assistant P.I. to the great Berkeley Barnes, I became a real split personality. In the *News* I was a guitar-playing freak, in the *Times*, a callow high school senior with his mouth slightly open. Oh well.

"Kathy has been so miserable. She cried and cried," said Isabel.

"*She* cried?"

"She felt so bad about not wanting you to stay at our place when your life was really in danger."

"Oh."

Isabel then started in on me about changing jobs. If I was going to be exposed to danger, I should be doing it in some worthwhile cause like picketing IBM, rather than risking my life for Consolidated's ill-gotten billions. I explained again about how ninety-nine percent of our work is nonviolent, dealing for the most part with very nice, friendly crooks who never lift a finger when they're caught.

After a half an hour of urging she became reconciled to my continuing. In return, I agreed to respect Bella Abzug.

Getting up the next morning wasn't as bad as I expected. Just half agonizing. After checking out of the hospital I took a cab home, showered, shaved, with some groaning, dressed, and tried to decide whether to go to work. Work won. Mainly because I was bored with the idea of lying around the apartment when things were going on at Consolidated which I should know about.

As Wickersham's representatives we had been relegated to a small office near Ryan's conference room. National Group had the conference room.

Barnes and Shunk were sitting in our inferior office. "I want you to get downtown and look at some pictures," said Shunk. "That Preeble broad says one of the Afros was exceptionally tall."

I shook my head, puzzled. "I didn't notice that."

He grunted. "All colored look alike to her. But one of them was very tall."

Ryan came in and congratulated me on being alive. I thanked him, with some reservations. All the time the City of New York was considering the legal ramifications of bailing me out with the hijacked money, good old Consolidated, with their billions, were sitting on their hands. Since I was working for them, you'd think they'd offer to ante up a miserable little hundred thousand. No thanks to Ryan that I was still alive.

Shunk said to Ryan, "Barnes here has the wild idea that the money is still here in the building."

"Not a wild idea. Completely logical," said Barnes.

Ryan stared at him. "What kind of malarky is this?"

"The money never left the building."

"Where, for God's sake? In the vault?"

Barnes shook his head. "Of course not. It left the vault, but it didn't leave the building."

"Ridiculous!"

"Doris Preeble was watching the street the whole time. The only possible answer is that the money is hidden here in the building. Or you're wrong, Rod, about the time you came downstairs. Could it have been before one-fifteen?"

Ryan rolled his eyes upward, disgusted. "No, I am not wrong about the time. I looked at my watch, wondering when the damned Denzer people were going to get here."

Shunk said, "I wouldn't trust that broad's testimony in a jaywalking case. She probably went to the bathroom and forgot all about it."

"How thoroughly did you search the building?" Barnes asked Shunk.

Shunk rubbed his chin. "Actually we searched it twice. The first go-round was to make absolutely sure none of the perpetrators were still on the premises. That was a hasty search, and we were only looking for armed strangers. The second search was thorough. We were looking for money."

"You had this possibility in mind?" asked Barnes.

Shunk seemed a little embarrassed, if you can imagine Shunk embarrassed. "No, actually not. Sometimes people take advantage of a situation like this. The vault was open. The thieves took a lot of money; they also left a lot of money. Who is going to miss another fifty thousand?"

Ryan began to redden. "Are you suggesting—"

Shunk held up his hand. "Not suggesting anything. We merely followed standard procedure. It has happened, you know. We collar the hoods, they say, 'We took five hundred and thirty thousand, three hundred and eighty dollars.' The loss is claimed as six hundred and ten thousand. The insurance company wants to know, you cops got sticky fingers or what?"

"Why believe a statement from a bunch of crooks?" asked Ryan.

Shunk shrugged. "In most cases they don't have much reason to lie about it. They get hung just as high for five hundred thousand as six hundred thousand. Anyway, as I said, it's standard procedure."

"I want another search," said Barnes. "A very thorough search."

"For God's sake, Berk. Shunk just told you they made a thorough search," said Ryan.

"Not thorough enough, evidently."

Ryan stomped to the door, then turned. "We're busy as hell. We're running about three days behind, a financially dangerous way for us to operate. In addition, everyone is on overtime. I strenuously object to this search. I will not tolerate it."

Barnes said, "We'll try wherever possible not to interfere with work."

Ryan threw up his hands. "You know everybody stops working if a cop as much as sticks his head in one of the offices. Be reasonable, Berk. I know you're teed off about being replaced, but don't take it out on me."

Barnes turned to Shunk. "I realize it's a grave inconvenience for Consolidated, but under the circumstances I must make a formal request, on behalf of Wickersham, that another search be carried out."

Shunk grinned at Ryan. "I guess they got a right to another search if they want it. It's their loss."

I could see Ryan doubling up and then undoubling his fists, which were hanging at his sides. "Their loss, my foot! When anything like this happens they triple their premiums and get back twice as much as they lost."

"When do you want to start, Berk?" Shunk asked Barnes.

"Immediately."

Ryan grunted disgustedly and was about to go through the door when a tall, gray-haired man clutching a battered black briar pipe in his jaw appeared. Ryan stepped aside for him to enter.

"Ah, Berk, they told me I'd find you here," he said, shaking hands with Barnes. Barnes then introduced him to me as Dale Jones, a vice-president of Wickersham. Ryan and Shunk he had met, of course.

Jones commiserated with me on my horrible experience, and indicated that he was pleased to find me whole and in fair health. They, Wickersham, were even inclined to overlook the irregularity of returning the money, which just might be part of the robbery loot, though, of course, he could not speak for their legal staff. All in clipped British prose formed by removing the pipe briefly and holding it toward me like a gift.

"If that was robbery loot, they had to change most of it into tens, which doesn't seem likely," said Shunk.

Ryan saw his opportunity and said, "Look Dale, Barnes here wants to make another search of the building, and—"

Jones waved his pipe, interrupting. "I know. We discussed the matter. A most intriguing idea."

"But—"

"Wouldn't it be absolutely smashing if we found the whole bloody kit and kaboodle right here in the building?" He pointed the stem of his pipe at Ryan. "Then we wouldn't have to raise your premiums, eh?" He yelped softly a few times, which was probably supposed to be a laugh.

"It's going to cost us a lot of money to have another day shot," said Ryan.

Jones became serious. "When I hire an expert, I follow his advice. I believe there's adequate reason to request another search. Sorry, Rod. We'll ask them to disrupt as little as possible." He jammed his pipe back in his mouth and began to emit great clouds of smoke.

Ryan shrugged and left.

Shunk said, "When you say 'immediately,' do you mean right this minute?"

"As soon as practicable," said Barnes.

"I'd like to bring the same team back. It will save a lot of time to know where they have already looked, and where they might have missed."

"Of course."

"Sergeant Carlucci was in charge. I believe the two patrolmen were Gaines and Steig." Shunk rubbed his chin. "I'll check with Carlucci and see how soon he can get them together."

"One man from the team would do it, if you can't pull them all in," said Barnes.

Carlucci was on another assignment, but Shunk managed to locate the two patrolmen who had made the earlier searches under Carlucci's direction. Their names were Gaines and Pagano; Steig had apparently only taken part in the first hasty search. They reported to Barnes about an hour later.

Pagano was open-faced, big-mouthed, and smiling. "I hear we got to take this joint apart *again*," he said.

Barnes hesitated. "Well, just what you missed. Assuming you missed something."

Gaines shook hands with me. He was a tall,

slender Negro. "I hear some of my soul brothers gave you a hard time."

"Yeah."

"I know that little bastard Spinoza. He's a real ripoff."

"I know him too. He was a good friend of mine in college."

Gaines looked at me closely, as though measuring me up carefully for his own wanted file. "He was? Well, man, you ought to be more careful about who you pick for friends."

Barnes had done some calculating about the size of the bundle we were looking for. It would have to contain, at a minimum, a single stack of bills about ninety inches high, or seven feet, six inches tall. It could be in any number of different shapes. Four stacks twenty-two and a half inches high, eight stacks eleven and a quarter inches high, and so on. In sixteen stacks it could make a package five and five eighths inches thick, twenty-one inches long, and twelve and one fourth inches wide.

"Keep in mind that they might have divided it into two or three smaller bundles," said Gaines.

"Quite possible."

"I suppose we start in the basement, where we did before?" asked Pagano.

"Logical," said Barnes.

The basement was relatively easy. The back half of it was taken up with the vault, and another quarter of it with the sparsely furnished

227

lobby outside the vault. The vault we could ignore. We assumed that the money had actually left it, and was not hidden in unopened cases of money orders or in some other "Purloined Letter" situation within the vault. If it had merely been hidden there, getting it out later would pose almost as many problems as a new robbery. Money could not be removed without at least three people inventorying it, and in actual practice there were usually four or five present when any sizable amount of money was removed. Of course, Ryan had the complete combination, but the presence of the time lock made it impossible for him to open the vault in an off hour when no other employees were around.

The smooth walls of the lobby and the unbroken plaster ceiling offered no place of concealment. The remainder of the basement was occupied by a large heating unit, an oil burner, janitorial equipment, and other odds and ends. We looked inside the oil burner, and inspected the large oil-storage tank.

"No chance, I suppose, of their wrapping the money in plastic and concealing it in the oil tank?" I asked.

Gaines shook his head. "Other than a small drain cock, the only entrance to the tank is the pipe which opens up at street level. Where they fill it."

"This is a hot-water system, isn't it?" asked Barnes.

Pagano said, "Yeah, baseboard radiators. They tore out all the old steam radiators when they made the house into an office building."

"At least we don't have hot-air vents to worry about," I said.

"Man, we'd need a heating engineer or plumber for that," said Gaines.

We inspected the mops, pails, brooms, and burlap trash sacks. You couldn't hide a half million dollars under a few mops. There was a coffee cart with a large urn. We looked into the urn. Nothing but coffee dregs. Aside from an inset fire hose, the smooth concrete wall was unbroken. We pulled the fire hose out and looked behind it. Nothing but dust. The floor was also concrete, and showed no break or evidence of tampering.

We moved up to the first floor. It consisted of five rooms plus a corridor. The reception area was about ten feet by fifteen, and was furnished with leather armchairs and a leather sofa. A small table, the receptionist's desk, and switchboard completed the furnishings. We looked at the sofa and chair cushions, inspected the undersides, went through the receptionist's desk while she stood by giggling, looked behind all the pictures for old safes which might have been left over from the day when the building was a rich man's mansion, and turned the carpet back to inspect the asphalt-tiled floor.

The room was lighted by fluorescent tubes set

into the ceiling of acoustical tiles. The lights were covered by large squares of white rippled plastic panes resting even with the ceiling.

Gaines saw Barnes studying the light fixtures. "We checked the space between the dropped ceiling and the real ceiling."

"How?"

"We took the cover off each light fixture, then poked with a stick, probing an area of three feet around each fixture. We figured if they stuffed the money up there, it would be done by opening one of the light fixtures."

Barnes nodded. "I'll accept that."

Pagano sighed audibly. "Glad we don't have to go through *that* again."

"Pagano got a shock, poking around in one of them."

"Knocked me right on my ass."

"The way he dived off that chair was something to see," said Gaines. "You might call it a backward swan dive."

Pagano raised his fists, shifted into a boxer's stance and offered to take Gaines on.

"One thing I hate about narc investigations. They hide the stuff in the electrical fixtures. I've gotten a couple of bad jolts myself," said Gaines.

Each room had a circular air conditioning vent in the ceiling. "Did you check those?" I asked, staring at the one overhead.

"We did, and they were real bitches," said Pagano. "We looked in all the ducts."

"Good," said Barnes. "We won't repeat that either."

I began to wonder whether the search would really turn up anything. The police had done a pretty thorough job. Certainly there were decided advantages to hiding the money in the building. Gates, Horgan, and Ryan were all under suspicion. Having the money in their possession, or say in a safe deposit box, would be dangerous and foolish. Hidden here, even if found, the money might not help us pin the crime on a specific individual. If we were unsuccessful, it could be left for months until the heat died down completely. Later, it could be carried out in small packets in briefcases, even pockets.

There were four more rooms on the first floor. One was a large, beautiful furnished office which had the air of being unused. It was, I found, maintained for General Ellsworth to occupy when he happened to be uptown. There was no bundle of money in this office, unless you considered the net value of the furnishings. Three of the paintings were Impressionist originals, worth many thousands.

Then we came to the men's room and the ladies' room. We sent one of the girls in to check whether the ladies' was empty, and then posted her outside to head off any customers. Both lavatories were largely tile and plumbing fixtures, and aside from two small doors, one in each, which led to pipe channels, there was no place to hide a bundle of money. Not any place that could be opened and closed up within a half hour. We shined lights up and down the pipe channels and found no indication that anything had been placed in them. The dust was thick and undisturbed.

The last room on the first floor was a combination mail sorting and storage facility. It was large, about twenty-five by thirty feet, and looked like a small post office. The thousands of stores in the area selling Consolidated money orders mailed in their receipts twice a week in special brown envelopes supplied by the company. Those envelopes were about nine inches by six inches in size, and routinely contained the duplicates of the money orders sold and the store owner or manager's check for the total sum taken in. Long wooden sorting tables, wall racks divided into numbered squares, and straight chairs were the only furnishings. There were scales, a Pitney-Bowes machine, several big canvas mail bags, and other pieces of mail room equipment, including three deep canvas-walled carts. Four clerks were busily opening envelopes and placing the contents in the numbered wall racks.

"Don't suppose our man could have stuffed about forty-five of those brown envelopes and buried then in the bottom of one of the canvas carts?" I asked. It would probably take longer than the allotted time. Still, working fast he, or they, could do it.

"Not unless the clerks were in on it," said Gaines. "These carts are being emptied and processed constantly."

"Suppose," said Barnes, "he already had forty-five of these envelopes addressed, with proper postage on them? Could he have filled them and dumped them into the outgoing mail?"

That stumped Gaines for a moment. Then he brightened. "No. Those brown envelopes are *incoming* things. The blank money orders:e are hand-delivered to the stores by Consolidated representatives. When they deliver a supply, they leave the store the brown envelopes to mail in the receipts. A large number being mailed out from Consolidated would be noticed immediately."

Barnes nodded. Gaines had done more than just search.

The back area of the room was obviously a storage area, with shelves of office supplies, forms, envelopes, and other materials. On the floor there were a number of large packages, about twelve inches by twenty inches in size and wrapped in heavy brown paper. They were stacked in neat rows.

"What are those?" I asked.

Pagano kicked one of them. "Canceled money

orders. They keep canceled money orders from the past six months upstairs. Each day, a day's supply which is then six months old is packaged and brought down here, leaving room for the current day's receipts to go into the files. About every three weeks these bundles of old money orders are trucked down to Consolidated's central headquarters, microfilmed, and then destroyed."

"I suppose you opened all the bundles when you searched?"

He picked up one and held a side up for me to see. It had a big D.A.'s office seal on it.

There were, of course, some new packages, since they were piling up every day. We opened all the unsealed bundles. As expected, they contained canceled money orders.

The corridor offered no hiding place, unless the perpetrator had had time to spread the bills under the carpeting, which was not likely. Anyway, the edges of the capeting showed no signs of having been disturbed.

We were heading for the second floor when we met Dale Jones near the steps. "Well, old boy, did you find it?" he asked Barnes.

"Not yet. So far we've only checked the basement and the first floor." He introduced Gaines and Pagano.

Jones shook hands with them. "Been giving it a bit of thought. I'm inclined more than ever to

234

agree with you. The money must be in the building."

"I don't think so," said Gaines bluntly.

"No? Why not?" asked Jones, turning to him.

"Because we searched *very* thoroughly right after the robbery."

"Hmmmm," said Jones, glancing at Barnes.

"Don't worry, it's here.'

"I hope so. Ryan's nose is very much out of joint. I'd hate to lose their business with Wickersham."

"Don't worry."

We started up the steps to the second floor, Jones accompanying us. It consisted of several executive offices and one large room containing about twenty desks for Consolidated's sales representatives and some of the secretaries. The numerous file cabinets in the big room took some time. Gaines admitted they had merely spot-checked here, opening every third drawer. We all pitched in and opened every drawer and riffled the contents looking for the green stuff.

Ryan was sitting at his desk when we reached his office.

"This room is next, Mr. Ryan," said Gaines.

Ryan looked at Barnes as though he might be a polluted lake, but said nothing. He got up quietly and left the office. I felt in my pockets for the Gelusil.

Out of the corner of my eye I saw Ryan take Dale Jones by the arm and walk him some ten feet away. Probably telling him about how they were going to change insurance companies.

Barnes, who misses nothing, accepted the Gelusil tablets I handed him and chewed them up thoughtfully.

Ryan's office was modern. He had an L-shaped desk with almost no drawer space, a comfortable sofa, and two leather armchairs. A heavily padded swivel chair, upholstered in matching leather, stood inside the L of the desk. There was no place to hide a bundle of money unless you ripped open a couple of the leather cushions. We inspected the seams of all the upholstery even though Gaines had, of course, done it earlier. The room's single closet had nothing in it but ordinary items. A plastic raincoat, an old briefcase, empty, two umbrellas, a tape recorder. On the top shelf there was a large bundle wrapped in brown paper.

"Did you open that?" I asked Gaines, pointing to the bundle.

He stared at it for a few seconds and then shook his head. "Wasn't there."

It turned out to be seven freshly laundered shirts.

We got equally interesting evidence in Gates's, Cressett's, and Tip Horgan's offices. For an heir apparent, Horgan's office was low on the status ladder. Scratched-up, worn oak furniture, mousy carpet with coffee stains, and papers stacked everywhere. In his closet, he lived well. There were three bottles of Jack Daniel's, a polo mallet, golf clubs, two large jars of expensive caviar, imported crackers, and eight cans of Coca-Cola.

"If he's mixing Jack Daniel's with that Coca-Cola, he's no friend of mine," said Barnes.

The third floor was divided into two huge rooms, each about forty by twenty feet. They contained nothing but special file cabinets, data-processing equipment, and desks.

Dale Jones decided he had had enough. "Well, chaps, I have a lunch date." He looked around at us vaguely and then said, "Good hunting."

We sent out for sandwiches and coffee, and ate and drank in one corner of the big room, eyed with considerable curiosity by the data-processing staff. When you search a building you've got to continue straight through. Theoretically, if you left for lunch, the bad guy could move what you were searching for into an area already searched. Not likely, in this case, with everyone at work, but we stuck to procedure.

The file cabinets were specially built. They had drawers about three inches deep and thirteen inches wide. A separation ran down the middle of each drawer, so that it could contain two rows of money orders filed by serial number, date, and data-processing group numbers. Each cabinet had twenty such drawers. Gaines told us there was a total of more than a hundred of those cabinets on this floor and the floor above. Consolidated sold approximately two million money orders per week in the metropolitan New York area. This meant that these files, which contained six months of canceled money orders, contained roughly *fifty million* pieces of paper. There were over two thousand drawers.

Some quick calculations indicated that the entire haul could fit into less than two drawers. Also, the money orders were only a sixteenth of an inch wider than paper money, and about the same height. Since the canceled money orders had seen considerable handling, they did not rest in even-edged rows by any means. If the thieves had used the back third of say, six drawers, the money would never be noticed when somebody merely pulled out the drawer and looked down at the top edges of the money orders. Six drawers out of two thousand!

"You checked these, of course," said Barnes. "How?"

Gaines looked uneasy. "We spot-checked a couple of drawers in each cabinet."

"Just looked at it?"

"We riffled one drawer in every cabinet."

"That's not enough of a sample. And I'm not sure you'd notice the difference if you just looked."

Gaines rubbed his chin. "I think you would. I'll admit the edges are the same sort of greenish

238

gray-white as money, but there's a slight difference in thickness that would show up. The amount of light reflected, you know."

Barnes nodded. "Possible. Let's find out for sure."

"Anybody got a stack of money about a foot high?" I asked.

Barnes turned to me, smiling. "This is one place where that won't be any problem."

He went down to see Gates and in about ten minutes came back with a canvas bag filled with stacks of one-dollar bills, half new and half used. We tried it three ways. We fitted in a stack of new bills, which were immediately noticeable with their smooth-edged neatness. The stack of used bills was very close in appearance to the money orders wedged on both sides, but there was a slight difference if you looked closely. The same was true when we mixed the old and new bills in a third twelve-inch stack.

"The stolen money was a mixture of old and new bills," said Barnes, "I suppose we can settle for just looking closely at each drawer."

Pagano groaned. "You mean we got to open all two thousand drawers?"

Barnes dumped the bills back into the canvas bags. "Why not? Allowing ten seconds per drawer, four of us can do it in about an hour and a half."

"I think fifty percent, selected at random, would be more than adequate," said Gaines.

Barnes glanced at his watch. "If we do it that way, and don't find the money, we'll have to go back and open all two thousand drawers. Including the ones we have already checked."

We opened two thousand drawers. Which I thought was a little unreasonable of Barnes. He was getting cracked on the subject of the money being there.

After all the drawer openings proved fruitless, we paused for coffee and sandwiches. There were still a lot of desks, computers, and ordinary file cabinets to go, plus the fifth floor.

At quarter of eleven we were up on the roof examining the air conditioning equipment with flashlights.

"Great place for hot money," said Gaines, happier now that he was being proved right. "Cool it right off."

Barnes muttered something under his breath. I examined my supply of medications and handed him a couple of tranquilizers.

"I know the money is in this damned building somewhere. I'd bet every cent I have in the bank on it," said Barnes. He chewed them up.

In a sense he was doing just that. Consolidated was sore at us. Now Wickersham would be sore. These were steady, bread-and-butter clients. Isabel and I might have to cop out in Spain earlier than we were financially ready for it.

"I'm going to find it if I have to take this building apart stone by stone," said Barnes.

Pagano sat down on the roof. I thought he was going to cry. Actually he just moaned and complained about how tired he was.

Barnes looked at him. "Oh, hell, we'll knock off. I've got to give this some more thought."

The next day was Saturday, and I was looking forward to spending it with Isabel. Barnes was not a happy substitute. He buzzed my apartment about nine o'clock and, thinking it might be Isabel, I let him in. His visit had a double purpose. He had a female beagle puppy in his topcoat pocket, which he wanted to provide with a home in my apartment; also he wanted to discuss his *idée fixe*, that the robbery money was still in the building.

I made a pot of coffee, backing away from beagle puppy ownership. I explained that while I love dogs I was simply not ready to accept the responsibility of walking, feeding, watering, housebreaking, and providing lots of love and affection for this cute little stray. She had no collar, no license. Barnes had found her grubbing around an overturned garbage can.

"If I turn her in, they'll dispose of her in a few days if no one adopts her," he said.

"Someone will adopt her."

He stared at me grimly. "You have a hard streak somewhere inside, don't you?"

"Look, you know from your work with the AGAS that there are literally thousands of animals in this condition."

He handed me the puppy. She licked my hand and stared up at me with her sad, bloodshot hound eyes.

"Look," I said, "maybe Isabel will take her."

I poured her a bowl of milk. She lapped it up eagerly. Then she went over to the stove and made a little puddle.

"You see?"

While I mopped up, he started in again about how the money had to be hidden in the building."

"But where, for God's sake?"

"It's there, dammit. I want to get hold of the plans of the building.

Hidden rooms? Hidden closets? He was really getting far out.

"Look, even if there is a hidden closet or something, it's plastered over. Not something someone could conceal the money in in a half hour."

"I want to see those plans."

If we were to get the plans, Dale Jones would have to make the request. Consolidated wouldn't cooperate with us to that extent.

He telephoned Jones at his home, and Jones agreed to meet us at his office at ten-thirty.

Wickersham's offices were all the way downtown in a tall building overlooking the Battery.

Puffing on his old briar, Jones was cool but not completely unfriendly. "I hope you know what you're doing, old boy. Ryan's tremendously annoyed. Claims they are having to work everyone overtime today to make up for work lost yesterday."

"He'll get over it. When we find the money."

Jones puffed some more. "If you're wrong, we may lose Consolidated's business when this is all over. Do you realize that they insure with us on a national basis? The amount of money involved?"

"General Ellsworth will be pleased when we clean it up. He's got a rotten apple there. The sooner we uncover it, the better he's going to like it," said Barnes.

Jones shook his head doubtfully. "Consolidated is our biggest customer on this side of the Atlantic. If you damage our business relationship, I'll guarantee you'll smart for it."

"Take a positive view. Think of how pleased the General will be when the money is recovered and his premium rates are maintained."

Jones knocked out his pipe. Taking a worn plastic pouch from his pocket, he began to carefully fill it.

"It's there," said Barnes. "If we don't find it, whoever stole it will be able to remove it bit by bit and you'll never recover a *dime*."

Jones jerked his head back slightly at the vehemence of Barnes's tone. He lit his pipe slowly until it was burning evenly.

"Just what do you want me to do? What good will the plans of the building do you?"

"I want the plans of the old mansion. It was converted to an office building in the thirties. If we can compare the difference in the layout of rooms and wall, we may hit on some beautifully simple hiding place we'd never notice in a search."

Jones got up and strolled to one of his large windows overlooking the harbor. An ocean liner was idling by.

"I see your point," he said, turning. "You know the official thinking is that Cressett got the money. That he tried to doublecross his underworld accomplices. They killed him. They have all the money."

"How do you account for the man Doris Preeble saw leaving? He locked the front door. He was carrying nothing."

"Cressett. The others went out the side door to the parking lot, Cresset locked up after them, then went out the front door."

"Why?"

"Probably didn't want to take a chance riding away in the getaway car with the money."

Barnes smiled. "If they had the money, how could Cressett double-cross them?"

Jones removed his pipe and studied it as though somebody might have put an old rubber band in his tobacco. Finally he shrugged. "Too deep for me, old boy."

"Will you ask General Ellsworth for the plans? I doubt if Ryan will cooperate."

He marched back to his desk and sat down. "I shall. That is, I'll try to get the plans, one way or another. Not necessarily through General Ellsworth."

"Good," said Barnes. "You won't regret it."

"Let's hope *you* won't regret it," said Jones.

Since there was nothing further for us to do but wait, Barnes suggested that I might want to take Saturday afternoon off. Big deal. I thanked him. He hasn't heard that everybody else in the civilized world works a five-day week.

I went home to Princess Running Waters, who had managed to leave a few more puddles around the apartment. I picked her up. "How could an animal as small as you are do so much? You must be seven eighths water." She licked my face and grinned at me.

After I finished cleaning up, I decided it was time to visit Isabel. Both of us.

Isabel was just leaving to go to the laundromat. "Oh, isn't it darling!"

"A little present for you," I said hopefully.

"For *me?*"

"Yep."

"Isn't it *sweet!*" She put down the laundry bag and cuddled Princess Running Waters. "I just love beagles."

"It's sure cute, all right."

She baby-talked the puppy for a while, making cooing sounds in between.

"It's too bad Kathy is allergic to dogs. I'd just love to keep it."

At that moment Kathy came into the living

room and saw the dog. She screamed, and then started sneezing violently.

I took Princess out into the hall.

"Of course, you could get another roommate," I said.

She just smiled. We went to the laundromat and washed her clothes.

I took the dog home, laid a thick carpet of newspapers in the kitchen, and closed her off in there. I thought I'd take a nap, since I had a couple of hours before meeting Isabel for dinner.

Scratch, scratch, scratch on the kitchen door. Whine, whine, whimper, whimper. An experimental bark or two. Howl. Have you ever heard a little beagle howl? Damn Barnes anyway. I opened the door. "Okay, you can come out if you promise not to do anything."

We had a hefty Italian dinner in the Village accompanied by a bottle of red wine, then went to a party given by some friend of Isabel's who worked in the same place she did. There were about fifty people crammed into an apartment which could have comfortably held twelve. The air was thick with pot, incense, and ordinary cigarette smoke, plus a few pipes. We fooled around, listening to albums and drinking cheap wine for a couple of hours, but the pot smoking made me nervous. Not only have I given it up, but if I got busted it would be very embarrassing to Barnes. Also I'd lose my P.I. license. I mean, why take a chance on getting busted for something you're not even doing?

We left and went to my apartment and listened to some John Mayall albums And played with Princess. Isabel didn't care for the name. We tried a lot of names out on Princess for size, including Bella, but we finally settled on Griselda. Don't ask me why. Probably because we got tired of the game at that point.

9

Nine A.M. Sunday morning and Barnes was buzzing for admittance. I released the downstairs lock, then went to the door.

"I'd invite you in, but it's sort of awkward," I said.

He was a bit taken aback. Then he smiled. "Oh, your girl friend is here."

"Well—"

"It won't embarrass me," he assured me.

I didn't think it would embarrass Isabel either, but why should he intrude upon our cozy breakfast?

"Actually I'm driving up to Cottonwood, Connecticut, to see General Ellsworth, and I thought you'd probably want to come along. I'll go have some coffee and pick you up in a half an hour."

Isabel wouldn't like it. But Barnes knows I'm too curious to want to miss any interesting developments.

"Okay. I'll be waiting down front."

Isabel didn't like it, and we had a mild argument. I always win by pointing out that I couldn't make this kind of bread clerking at

Korvette's, which is probably what I would be doing.

Cottonwood is an exclusive little commuter village about an hour's drive from New York. An hour if you drive as fast as Barnes does in his Porsche. The homes start at about a hundred thousand dollars for a cheapie and go up from there. Ellsworth would probably have some place.

"Have you been to his home before?" I asked.

Barnes hit a long straightway and went up to a hundred. I tightened my seat belt. "We're not going to his home. I'm going to try to buttonhole him at church."

"Church?"

The speedometer eased down to eighty and I felt a little better. "Late yesterday afternoon Jones called me with a long song and dance about there being no plans. It seems that the mansion was originally built in 1890. In 1932, when it was made into an office building, no one could locate the original plans. The architect was long dead. The city files were incomplete due to a fire or something."

"How about the architect who modernized it?"

We were creeping up to ninety. "Also dead. We can check the firm, but not until Monday."

"How come you're going to see him at church?"

"He might not see me at home. I remembered

that he was quite a wheel in the Presbyterian Church. With luck, he'll be there and perhaps I can ask him a few questions."

Barnes saw a cruising patrol car ahead and slowed down to seventy.

"If he's not there, we'll try his home."

We asked in a gas station, and found the Cottonwood Presbyterian Church without difficulty. Barnes's hunch about the General had been correct. He was not only attending, he was ushering. We found him standing in the narthex, outside the double doors leading into the church, a stack of church calendars in his hand. They are really programs, but they call them calendars for some reason or another. It was a real formal church. He and the other ushers were dressed in striped pants and tails.

"Ah yes, Berkeley Barnes," he said, offering his hand. "So nice to see you. Didn't know you lived up in this neck of the woods."

He turned to me. "And this is our assistant. Don't tell me, let me think." I let him think, but my name continued to escape him.

"Where would you like to sit, down front? We don't have reserved pews any more, you know. You can sit anywhere."

That was my biggest thrill of the morning. Barnes said, "I don't live up here, General. I was hoping to have a few words with you about the Consolidated robbery."

He frowned. A family group, mother, father,

251

and two girls, came up behind us. He smiled at them, and we stood aside while he guided them down to seats. When he returned he said softly, "We can't discuss it here. I'll be too busy greeting people and seating them. Then we take up the offering—" Some new arrivals interrupted us. He beamed, shook hands with them, and guided them down to seats. When he returned he said, "I'm afraid you'll have to wait until the service is over."

The minister was a nice young guy with mod longish hair. In his sermon he mentioned how the congregation should try to get more black people to attend, and how they should be made welcome in Cottonwood, and that homeowners shouldn't band together to keep them from buying houses and all that sort of thing.

We were in the last row of pews, and General Ellsworth was standing a couple of feet away behind us. I heard him mutter to one of the other ushers, "Seedy-looking young pup, isn't he?"

I consulted the calendar-program and discovered the minister was only a guest minister. The regular minister probably didn't advise them to sell their three-hundred-thousand-dollar homes to Negroes. I mean, when one gets in, they just take over, and pretty soon all the big estates would be bought by Negroes.

When the service ended, the General came over and said, "Step out to my car and we'll have a chat."

A circular drive approached one of the church's entrances. Ellsworth's long black Fleetwood Cadillac was waiting right in front, at the head of a line of similar chauffeur-driven limousines. We climbed in the back. I sat sideways on one of the fold-down seats to give the General and Barnes plenty of room.

"Just pull over into the parking lot so we won't block traffic," Ellsworth said to the chauffeur. "We want to have a bit of a talk, and these gentlemen are probably going to head back to New York." Well, I didn't really expect for us to be invited to Sunday dinner, but he might at least have invited us over for a drink. I enjoy looking at sheer wealth, and I would have liked to see his estate.

"Just what is your interest, Mr. Barnes? I understood that we had retained National Group."

"Wickersham has hired me to continue my investigation."

He stared at us, his neatly clipped gray mustache framing the top of his slightly opened mouth. "Oh," he said.

Barnes quickly outlined our problem, and didn't spare the old man with diplomacy. The robbery was not only an inside job, but he was very much afraid either Gates, Ryan, or even Tip Horgan might well be involved. He outlined all his reasons for believing that the money was still hidden in the Consolidated building.

The General listened attentively. When he

finished, Barnes fished out his cigarettes and lit one. I made a note to remind him to enter it in his book later. He belatedly offered the package to Ellsworth.

Ellsworth shook his head slightly. "Thanks, no. Gave them up when I was seventy-five." His expression was moodily blank. We waited while he pondered. Some teen-age boys with shoulder-length hair passed the car walking through the parking lot. "Disgusting. Rotten little wretches look like girls," said Ellsworth.

After another moment he said, "This is appalling. I find it extremely difficult to accept." He bent his head wearily and rubbed his forehead. "Next year Consolidated will be one hundred years old. Since its founding there has been an Ellsworth in the management. We've had disasters, heavens yes. But nothing like this. And under my stewardship—"

"The quicker it is resolved, the quicker the slate will be wiped clean," said Barnes.

Ellsworth sighed. "I'm not sure, I even care. Anyway, the slate will never be wiped clean if it's one of my top people." He gestured toward Barnes. "I believe I shall have one of your cigarettes."

Barnes shook one out of his package and offered it to Ellsworth.

"Symptomatic of the times, I suppose," said Ellsworth, accepting a light from Barnes. "Do you know that people use our money orders to evade income taxes? They receive cash that they can juggle from their businesses or professions. They dare not put it in a bank or a safe deposit box. Keeping large sums of cash in the home is dangerous. They buy our money orders and hide them away."

"Indeed?" said Barnes.

"Prostitutes use our money orders. After they finish 'turning a trick' as I believe they call it, they buy a money order and mail it to themselves. That way the pimp doesn't get his hands on as much as he would like to."

"Hmmmm," said Barnes.

"The sad part of it is, we make more money when people hide our money orders away for illegal purposes. Our float is bigger."

"Float?" I asked.

"Investable balance, young man. We take in money, we pay out money, usually almost as fast as we take it in. Money orders that are hidden for months or years give us months and years of investment of that capital."

I was learning things about the money-order business.

Barnes tried to get us back on the track. "I understand the plans of the original mansion have been lost. Your midtown headquarters?"

"Ah, yes. But as I was saying, this corruption is symptomatic of the times. Pornography flourishes, crime is rampant, homosexuality is flaunted, women are brazen, showing off their private parts in public. Why, I saw a motion picture recently—well, good taste forbids my describing it to you. Sufficient to say that it wouldn't have been tolerated as a stag show in my day.'

"The mansion, do you remember it?"

"Remember it? Scott's Emulsion, how would I ever forget it? You wouldn't know about the Depression of the early thirties," he told me, "But let me tell you, my Uncle Ted was very happy to get out from under that white elephant."

"The original mansion was your uncle's home?"

"Indeed it was. I spent many happy childhood hours there with my cousins. My own home was nearby, over on Fifth Avenue."

Barnes lit another of his cigarettes, unnoted. He was really slipping. "Perhaps if we could persuade you to stroll through the building you might remember the original arrangement of walls, rooms, and closets. Knowing the house, a natural hiding place might occur to you."

The General smiled wearily. "Young man, do you know that I am seventy-eight years old? It's been more than sixty years since I played there with my cousins. It has been an office building for almost forty years."

Barnes refused to give up. "Still, childhood memories can come back vividly at times."

Ellsworth sat thinking. After a while he mur-

mured, "Hiding places—Scott's Emulsion, where would you hide a half million dollars?"

Some more long-hair kids walked through the parking lot. Ellsworth spotted them. "Idle hands. They don't get proper discipline, that's the problem. Their parents are too lazy to keep them properly busy."

Barnes said, "The mansion must have been a very pleasant and spacious house."

Ellsworth chuckled. "Lord, yes. Speaking of discipline, got the worst thrashing of my life in that house. Father, Mother, brother Albert, and I were there for Sunday dinner. Albert and I, and our two cousins, Billy and Quincy, decided it would be interesting to fill rubber balloons with water and drop them down the laundry chute. I assure you, I can remember the hiding my father gave me to this day."

I laughed politely. Barnes sat up straighter and said loudly, "Laundry chute!"

Ellsworth was startled. After a few seconds, he shook his head. "Wouldn't be there. I'm certain it was either torn out or walled over in thirty-two. If I remember correctly, it terminated in the section of the basement which is now the vault. I assure you there's no laundry chute opening in that vault. If it's there, there's eight inches of steel and concrete over it."

"There might be an opening on one of the other floors."

"Probably all walled over. Otherwise, one would recall seeing it."

Barnes was getting desperate. "How about fireplaces and chimneys? There must have been a number of fireplaces."

"All sealed up tight with brick, mortar, and concrete."

"I know it's an imposition, general, but would you come with us and look the place over? If we looked around a bit I'm sure you'd remember other things," said Barnes.

Ellsworth thought it over. "Why not? I have nothing ahead of me but luncheon, which will consist of chicken soup, graham crackers, a glass of milk, Jell-O. For the rest of the afternoon my treat will be the one cigar I'm allowed. Can't read the *Times* any more. Pushes my blood pressure sky-high."

I stifled a laugh. Barnes allowed a decent interval of sympathetic silence to elapse, then made arrangements to meet the General at Consolidated's offices at two-thirty. Seems that if he didn't go home and eat the graham crackers, Mrs. General would hide his cigars.

As we eased out of the Fleetwood, the visiting minister passed on the way to his own car. Ellsworth lowered his window and said loudly, "Get a haircut. Be a *man!*"

On the way back we paused for a martini and a quick lunch. Barnes called Shunk to make it official. When Shunk heard that Ellsworth was

258

going to be there, he decided it was worth his Sunday afternoon to make an appearance.

The General was only ten minutes late. Would have been on time but the confounded soup was too hot. Take the skin right off your lips if you eat it too fast. Barnes introduced Shunk, and Patrolman Madden, who was watching the store.

"As yes, Lieutenant Shunk," said Ellsworth. "Your commissioner is a lily-livered ass. Old friend of mine." He paused for a moment to stare sternly at Shunk. "Barnes here has probably mentioned it to you, we're going to try to take a little trip down memory lane."

"Yes, General," said Shunk, actually smiling. "The laundry chute sounds interesting."

During our search, I had seen no indication of a laundry chute opening anywhere. It could have been covered by file cabinets.

"General, perhaps we could start by checking the probable location of the laundry chute on each floor. For openings," said Barnes.

Ellsworth was looking around with a bemused expression on his face. He faced Barnes. "Yes, of course. But you must remember that I have been seeing this house as a place of business for so many years. It is difficult to think back to when it was Uncle Ted's home. Many of the interior walls were shifted to provide areas suitable for business needs. The corridors are not the same." He walked down the hall a few paces and then returned. "Heavens, I can't remember where the original hall was that ran to the back of the house. It has to be in the back of the house. It must be in the sorting room."

We all walked back to the mail room, except Madden, who remained on duty at the door.

Ellsworth pointed to an area of wall flanked by two shallow cupboards. "That would seem to be the most obvious location. You can see that the cabinets are flush with the wall in the center. Built to even out a bulge, so to speak."

Why hadn't we noticed it? Who would think of a laundry chute?

Shunk rapped the wall with his knuckles. Good solid plaster. He moved to another area of wall and rapped for comparison. It sounded the same.

He smiled. "I would say this opening could not have been penetrated and repaired in a half hour."

"Hardly," said Ellsworth.

We measured the distance from the left wall to the laundry chute. Five feet.

On the second floor the laundry chute was located in Cresset's office. Solid plaster. A closet had been built on one side.

On the third floor we had to move some file cabinets. Solid plaster.

The fourth floor was more interesting. Here the entire wall was smooth, with no rectangular bulge. Attached to the wall was a large bulletin board covering the chute area. it was fastened with screws spaced along its border.

While Shunk went to his car to look for a screw driver, I started working on them with my small pocket knife. Once started, they unscrewed easily. They certainly hadn't been in there since 1932. Or two months ago.

I had six of the ten screws out by the time Shunk returned. We finished quickly and lowered the large, heavy board to the floor and shifted it to one side. The old wooden door was still there, unplastered. Only the knob had been removed. I inserted my knife blade in the crack and pried the door open.

We crowded around to look in. All we could see was cobwebs and gray painted wood lining the channel. I stuck my head in and got some cobwebs in my hair. About four inches down from the bottom of the door, a nail had been driven into the front wall.

"That nail looks new," I said.

Shunk looked in, then reached down and felt the nail. "It is new," he said, straightening up. "No corrosion."

Barnes said, "Suppose the thief wanted to lower the robbery package to the bottom of the chute for safekeeping? Possibly the nail was put in to have something to tie the cord to."

"Scott's Emulsion!" said Ellsworth. He looked in. "But there's no cord."

Barnes shrugged. "Maybe he got panicky and dropped the cord too."

Shunk went to telephone for reinforcements. The chute was fifty feet deep, and you couldn't see more than three feet down because of the cobwebs. They reflected the flashlight beam, providing a cloudy wall of impenetrable gray cotton. What we needed was a strong light with a fifty-foot cord.

We stood around speculating on how we would get the money up until some police technicians arrived. Pagano was in charge.

He grinned at me. "No rest for the wicked. How did we miss it?"

We watched while they lowered a two-hundred-watt bulb attached to a heavily insulated cord. The cop handling the wire backed away, clawing cobwebs out of the way with his hands and looked in. "Hell, I can't see a goddamned thing. Looks like a burlap sack down there."

"Full of money," I said.

"Who knows."

We all took turns looking. It was a burlap sack all right, and it covered the entire bottom.

"Grappling hooks?" asked Barnes.

"Hell, we got no grappling hooks that would fit into this thing," said Pagano. The shaft, I estimated, was about eighteen inches wide by twelve deep.

"Of course, we could cut through the wall of the vault," I said, more to relieve the monotony than anything else.

"Very funny," said Shunk.

"You got a real skinny cop? We could lower him to the bottom."

Shunk snapped his fingers. "Trespin!"

"Yeah," said Pagano.

The rest of us looked blank. "Trespin is a midget. We use him once in a while. A child gets stuck in a small place, things like that."

Shunk went downstairs to telephone, the switchboard being closed. The General decided to go to his office and nap, since locating Trespin would take some time. We promised to call him.

We pulled out some chairs, made ourselves comfortable, and waited. This business is a lot like the Army. Hurry up and wait.

Luckily Trespin wasn't visiting his old auntie in Sioux Falls. He made the scene in a little over an hour, the smallest midget I have ever seen. A midget's midget. A three-year-old with an adult's head and a nasty scowl.

The General, who had been called, turned to me and said in a low voice, "I haven't seen one of those little fellows since the press people sat one on old J. P. Morgan's lap forty years ago. You wouldn't remember it, but there was a Senate investigation—"

"I've seen the famous picture," said Barnes.

Trespin was standing on a chair and peering down the shaft. He straightened up and turned to face us, a tiny orator ready to address a crowd of five thousand. "I'm not going down there. Too many spiders. Can't stand spiders."

Shunk scratched his chin. "We could lower a mop or something and sort of clean them out."

Trespin shook his head. "Nope. If there were some kid down there hurt or maybe scared to death, I'd do it. But just to bring up a bundle of money—heck, you can get it up some other way."

The General strolled over to him. "I imagine you are well remunerated for this type of work?"

Trespin looked blank.

"You get paid for it," I translated.

Trespin's face cleared. "Yeah. Fifty bucks minimum. But I don't want this job. Fifty feet down in that shaft. Spiders. Bad air at the bottom. No sir. You can pay my cab fare from Brooklyn and back and we'll call it square."

Ellsworth cleared his throat. "We're rather anxious to resolve this matter this afternoon. Suppose I added a one-hundred-dollar bonus to your fifty?"

Shunk said, "How about that! A hundred-buck bonus."

"Can't stand spiders."

"Listen, we'll attach a cord to one of those big brooms and work it up and down until we get rid of the cobwebs," said Shunk.

Barnes said, "The whole job won't take more than five minutes."

"A hundred and fifty dollars for five minutes," I said.

Trespin remained silent, his unhappy face working.

"That's thirty dollars a minute."

Finally he said, "Okay, but you got to clean those spiders out. There's nothing more repulsive to me than spiders."

Two of the cops worked for a while cleaning the shaft with a couple of mops tied to cords, dropping them to the bottom and pulling them up. Eventually Trespin was satisfied, and climbed into the small rope harness they had constructed for him. He was gently lifted over the edge of the entrance, and they began to slowly lower him to the bottom.

The rope slackened. Trespin was on the bottom. His voice came up, faint but shrill. "Pull me up! Pull me up! This place is filthy with spiders!"

Shunk bent into the opening. "Grab the sack, and we'll pull you up."

"Get me up! Pull me out of here!"

"Be sure to bring the sack!" yelled Shunk.

"Pull me up or I'll *kill* you!"

The cops holding the ropes began tugging him upward. In a few seconds his head appeared above the bottom of the shaft doorway.

One of the cops grabbed under his miniature arms and lifted him out. He was clutching the large burlap sack. A black walnut-sized spider was perched on his head, another was scurrying along his arm.

"Get them off me!" he screamed. "Get them off me!"

They brushed him off.

The sack was empty.

No one could believe it. The two-hundred-watt bulb was lowered again, in case the money had dumped out on the way up, or had been merely resting under the sack. We again took turns peering down. Nothing but smooth gray boards.

From his expression, Barnes might have been watching them amputate his own arm. I dug around for the tranquilizer container and quickly handed him two pills. He stuck them in his jacket pocket, too stunned to even notice.

"Well," said Shunk, "that takes care of the laundry chute. Any other ideas, General?"

Barnes recovered. "The money was obviously hidden here first. It has been moved, or it has already left the premises."

"Hasn't left the premises. We've been checking every package larger than a number ten envelope," said Shunk.

"Barnes, I'm afraid you're flogging a dead horse," said Ellsworth. He rubbed his forehead wearily. "While I was trying to rest, I gave the matter considerable thought. Couldn't think of another place near big enough."

Barnes said, "The nail was placed there recently, the screws were loose."

"Maybe it's you that's got some screws loose," said Shunk, then barked a few times to show it was all in fun.

Trespin said to the General, "You want to pay me now, or do I have to send you a bill?"

Ellsworth smiled. "Come down to my office and I'll write you my personal check."

"I'd like to get the plans from the architectural firm that handled the redesign of the inside of the building," said Barnes.

Ellsworth stared at him. "Oh heavens, Barnes—" He turned and marched off.

Barnes turned to Shunk. "Otto, you *know* there's something peculiar about that laundry chute. The fact that it has been opened recently."

Shunk was feeling pretty happy, an unusual condition for him. He hadn't been aced out by the famous private eye finding the money, which had been right under the nose of the police, so to speak. "Well, Berk." He drew out the "Well." "I just don't know. There could be some reasonable explanation for it. Some repairman might have thought it was a channel for pipes or wiring. Who knows?"

"He wouldn't have driven a nail into the wall of the shaft."

He put his arm around Barnes's shoulders jovially. "Come on and I'll buy you a drink. I'm off

267

duty." He looked in my direction. "You too." He headed toward the stairs. "There could be some very simple explanation for that nail. I just can't think of one at the moment."

We made our way to a bar on nearby Madison Avenue and settled into a booth, Shunk on one side, Barnes and I on the other. Shunk ordered Jack Daniel's and Coca-Cola, Barnes and I ordered Scotch on the rocks.

"You mix Jack Daniel's with Coca-Cola?" asked Barnes, unwilling to believe it.

Shunk nodded. "Used to be a rye-and-ginger-ale man. Somehow I got switched to bourbon and Coke."

Barnes sighed. "Oh well," he said. It was pointless to argue about it. Forgive and forget.

"You got anything new on Ryan that you'd be willing to reveal to a private eye about to be defrocked through lack of customers?" Barnes asked.

Shunk smiled. "Don't take it so hard, Berk. You just go off half cocked once in a while. You play hunches too much." The waiter arrived with our drinks. Barnes averted his eyes while Shunk poured the jigger of Jack Daniel's into the Coke. "Ryan's just about the cleanest guy I have ever had checked out in my life. He and his family live well within their means, he has no expensive tastes or hobbies. No women, no gambling, no playing the market. Saves his money and goes to Mass every Sunday. If he had any part in this robbery, it would be a very great surprise to me. A very great surprise."

"Hmmmm. Anything new on Tip Horgan or Gates?"

"Nothing on Tip. We got nothing against consenting adults as long as they don't get violent. People worry about kids. Hell, most of these guys don't fool around with kids. Child molesters are rarely homos."

"I didn't mean that. I meant anything new on his possible connection with the robbery."

"Nary a new," said Shunk, lifting his drink. "Mud in your eye."

"Cheers." Barnes didn't sound cheers cheerfully. He took a drink of his Scotch moodily, and I followed suit. It was getting to be a long day, and I wondered what Isabel was doing.

"Now Gates. That guy bugs me. We don't have anything on him. But there's something definitely phony about that meeting with Spinoza McWilliams."

"He wasn't there to talk about a little ten-thousand-dollar embezzlement," I said. "Why meet in Grand Central? He would have just gone up to Harlem to see him. What could he do anyway, now that the case has gone to the .A.?"

Shunk took another gulp of his Coke and bourbon. "That's right. What the hell could he negotiate? We'll prosecute the broad. If we ever catch up with her."

"It's very strange, all right," said Barnes.

"The truth of the matter is that we haven't got an iota of evidence against anybody. Not a damned thing to connect them with this specific crime. The only evidence we've got is against a corpse. Cressett."

"Framed," said Barnes.

"So you say."

The waiter came over and we ordered another round.

"I know you think I'm becoming unbalanced on the subject, but the money is still in the building. Get those plans for me. You can ask for them officially," Barnes said.

"Oh, come on, Berk. Cut it out, will you?"

"As a personal favor?"

Shunk fiddled with his new drink. "Oh, hell. All right, I'll ask for them."

From that point on the conversation deteriorated into a discussion of Shunk's dog, which reminded me that I was a reluctant dog owner.

"You've got to find a home for that puppy," I said. "Isabel can't take her. Her roommate Kathy is allergic to dogs."

"I can't help it if your girl friend's roommate is a psycho," said Barnes.

The waiter came over. "Let me have the check," said Barnes.

"No indeed. My party," said Shunk.

"Otto, put your money away. This can go on

my expense account. You can't put it on yours."

"Sure I can. You look like a couple of lousy informers to me," said Shunk, grinning. He let Barnes pay, however.

I was hoping Barnes would call it a day. There was still time to have dinner with Isabel, provided she hadn't gone to a meeting of her Ralph Nader for President Club. No luck.

"I think we'll go have a talk with Gates."

"Before dinner, or after?" I asked. Working overtime, I figure I'm entitled to a free dinner. Barnes being a gourmet, we dine very well when he's buying.

Barnes glanced at his watch. "It's only six-thirty. We can think about dinner later."

We took a cab to Brooklyn Heights.

Mrs. Gates answered the door. She was a plump, placid little woman with gray hair and a quizzical look on her face. Barnes explained who we were.

"Come in. Dave's watching television." She turned and called, "Dave. Company."

When Gates saw us he got up and switched off the television set. He came into the hall and shook hands with us both.

"Sorry to disturb your Sunday evening," said Barnes.

"That's okay. Come in." He wasn't particularly happy to see us.

The apartment was neat, spic and span, and

271

comfortably furnished, though not by Sloane's by any means.

"If we're going to talk business, we'd better go back to my den. My bride's favorite program comes on in ten minutes."

We followed Gates down the hall to his den, a small room with a desk, a couple of chairs, and a studio couch. A portable television sat on the desk; there were a few books in a small bookcase, but the shelves were mostly filled with odds and ends.

Gates pointed to the chairs and eased himself onto the studio couch, putting his legs up. "Got a bad leg," he said. "Gives me fits when it's going to rain."

We sat down, pulling the chairs around to face him.

"So what's new? Understand you're working for Wickersham now."

Barnes nodded. "I wanted to talk to you some more about your meeting with Spinoza McWilliams."

"Oh, Christ."

"The whole business smells phony as hell. How could you negotiate on the Perez embezzlement? A complaint has already been filed."

He shifted his leg and groaned softly. "There are ways around it. Would you like a drink, or coffee?"

"No, thanks," said Barnes.

He looked at me. "How about you?"

272

"I'll pass too.'

There was a long silence while Barnes stared at Gates. Finally Gates shifted uncomfortably. "Listen, can I tell you something in absolute confidence? Ryan has ordered me not to discuss it with you, or anybody, for that matter. But I'm inclined to take a chance."

10

"If it doesn't concern the robbery, of course," said Barnes.

"This concerns my meeting with Spinoza. But it doesn't concern the robbery."

"By all means, let's discuss it."

"I have your word that you won't pass this on to Shunk?"

Barnes nodded.

"Last month we had blank money orders with a face value of more than two million dollars hijack ed from one of our armored trucks in Chicago."

"I remember."

"Our money orders have a maximum face value of one hundred dollars. Per money order, that is. In order to get the two million, the thieves would have to cash twenty thousand money orders for the full hundred dollars."

"Quite a project."

"You can say that again. But we're in even worse shape, of course. We've got to notify stores all over the country of the stolen serial numbers. Every fraudulent one cashed has to be followed up, by both the local police and our security people. Storekeepers lose confidence in our money orders and are afraid to cash them. Some decide they don't even want to *sell* them, and we lose agents. When they hear about a big robbery it reminds them that having money orders in their stores may spark a holdup or burglary."

"I believe I will have that drink," said Barnes. He had already jumped to the end of the story.

Gates got up slowly. "Scotch?"

"Fine."

He went to the door and called to his wife. "Dear, will you bring us three glasses and some ice?"

"Before, we never had much financial paper stolen. It caused a real hassle with our insurance company."

"Wickersham?" I asked.

"No. We had our blank financial paper insured with one of the Lloyd's group. They were giving us pretty reasonable rates because they figured they didn't stand to lose too much. You see, legally, a money order is a presigned check. It is no good until it is delivered."

"How do you mean?"

He limped over to a closet, opened it, and brought down a bottle of Haig. "Take an extreme case. Suppose I made out my personal check to you for one thousand dollars, signed it, and put it in a drawer in my desk. You take it when my back is turned and cash it. You've stolen it, in effect, and it is not a legal check. Not until I *give* it to you. Theoretically, whoever cashes it is stuck. You can litigate up and down the line and all over the place. Theoretically, any store or hotel that cashes one of our stolen money orders is stuck.'

His wife brought the glasses and ice, and Gates poured generously.

"So this insurance company takes a look at the situation they've gotten themselves into. Twenty thousand hundred-dollar checks, each one of which may require litigation if they proceed with their theory that the casher is liable."

"Thanks," said Barnes, accepting the glass Gates handed him.

"So they canceled our policy."

"Just like that."

"Not even a 'Sorry, old boy, shall we try for a higher rate?' "

I thanked him for the drink he handed me. "Really ran scared?"

"Scared is an understatement. They were so scared they were furious. Downright insulting."

"So Spinoza was the go-between," said Barnes.

Gates sipped his drink. "Yeah. You can see how we would be willing to pay a hundred thousand to get those twenty thousand pieces of paper back. What a mess!"

"You recovered the blank money orders?"

Gates chuckled. "We did. But as you know, Spinoza didn't get the money. For a couple of days there we lived in mortal terror, expecting a bomb through the front door."

"*You* lived in mortal terror," I said.

He looked at me apologetically. "Yeah, well—"

"You didn't deliver that money to the locker. I was following you."

"Indeed I didn't. You think I'm going to lug a hundred thousand dollars around New York? I had a couple of our armed guards in plain clothes deliver it and bring me the key."

"Why didn't you ante up another hundred thousand and get us both off the hook?"

"Why didn't you mind your own business, instead of getting us all fouled up?" He frowned into his drink. "What a goddamned eager beaver. Who do you think you are, Jesse James or something?"

We finished our drinks, thanked him, and left.

No cabs seemed to be cruising, so we had to take the subway back. Barnes was moody. I don't have any pills for that condition.

"How about dinner?"

Barnes looked at his watch. "Only . seven-thirty. As a matter of fact, I have a dinner date at eight-thirty."

"Oh."

"Let's make one more call." He got out a notebook, not the one in which he records his cigarette consumption. He flipped the pages. "Carpenter Meret."

"Who?"

"The fellow who had the fight with Tip Horgan."

We found a phone booth and Barnes dialed. Our witness was at home. He would see us if we didn't mind the appearance of his apartment, which was a shambles.

Carpenter Meret was enduring a jumbo hangover, and he wasn't kidding when he said the place was a shambles. Overflowing ashtrays, dirty glasses littering the floor, tables, chair arms; platters of food nine tenths empty, small plates with scraps. Wine spills on the rug. The lingering aroma of pot.

"Had a few friends over last night," he said, holding his forehead. "Just got up."

"I can see you're suffering. We won't keep you long," said Barnes.

Meret lit a cigarette, his hand trembling.

"About the brawl you had with Tip Horgan."

"He wants to settle out of court?" Meret asked. A look of hope glimmered through his pain.

"No, I just wanted to talk to you about it."

Hope died, leaving only unmitigated pain. "So what is it?"

"You say he threw the first punch?"

"Yep."

"You gave him quite a beating."

"I gave him quite a beating? Man, I was hardly able to lay a fist on him. Of course I was pretty loaded. Hell, he had already been in one fight. Either a fight or an auto accident."

279

"Already banged up, eh?"

"Is he saying I beat him up?"

"No. We didn't know he'd been in another fight."

Meret chain-lit a new cigarette from the butt he had been smoking. "He'd been in something. His face looked like a lawnmower had run over it. Later I figured that was why he was so touchy."

He was fumbling around for Alka-Seltzer when we left, thanking him.

Barnes said he had to run to make his dinner date. "Put your dinner on expense account," he said.

That was a disappointment. Five bucks was the standard for overtime dinners if not entertaining a client. Eating with Barnes, the check would be about thirty-five dollars for the two of us. If there was any justice in the world, I should charge up an eighteen-dollar dinner with wine. Which would make him very testy.

I decided to go home and put a pizza in the oven. What the hell. Barnes could pay five bucks for that pizza. I doubted if Isabel would still be there, or even at her own apartment. I was tired, and decided I wouldn't pursue the matter by telephoning.

Griselda had chewed up all the newspapers I had put down in the kitchen, and had spread the scraps equally throughout the living room, bedroom and bath. I was getting a bit irritated with Barnes. He might just find the little mutt scotch-taped to his front door.

I put a pizza in the oven, then cleaned up the mess, including a few places she had puddled and been careful not to do it on the paper.

I poured a glass of red table wine, and decided to have the pizza plain. The anchovies made it too salty. I remembered how thirsty I had been when I went to the meeting the night of the robbery. Parched, and the damned Coke machine wasn't working.

The Coke machine! We hadn't checked it. Gaines had opened it during their earlier search. But suppose our thief had first hidden the money in the laundry chute. Lowered it to the bottom on a long cord and then fastened the end of the cord to our famous nail. Then, later, moved it to the Coke machine? But why would he do that? Discovery would be much less likely in the laundry chute.

Still, it was another possibility. I'd mention it to Barnes.

I ate the pizza, read parts of the Sunday *Times*, had two more glasses of wine, and went to bed. Three drinks and three large glasses of wine and I got relaxed.

Persistent ringing finally penetrated my sound, wine-induced slumber. I flicked on the lamp and glanced at my watch as I lifted the receiver. Three-thirty. It was Barnes.

"The Coke machine," he said. Not 'Hello, Larry, sorry to wake you up,' or anything a decent human being would say.

"I know,' I said, "And I thought of it long before three-thirty in the morning. But why would he move it to the Coke machine? It would be much safer in the laundry chute."

"I can think of a reason."

Barnes sounded a little slurry. Who wouldn't be, spending the evening with a long, leisurely dinner at, say, Pavillon, with the right wine for every course, then a few more drinks with friends in some elegant apartment on Sutton Place? So around 3 A.M. he says to himself, "By George, I'll bet it's hidden in the Coke machine. I'll have to telephone my faithful slave, Larry Howe, and apprise him of this."

"Well," I said, "we ought to check into it first thing in the morning."

"Morning! I'm going to take a look right now."

I wanted to go back to sleep. Maybe I could hang up and pretend the phone had suddenly gotten out of order?

"There won't be anybody there but Tomlinson and the cop on duty. They won't even have the keys to the machine."

"That's no problem."

He then disconnected, first suggesting that I

be down in front of my apartment building in ten minutes, where he would pick me up.

On the East Side, Manhattan is pretty deserted at 3:30 A.M. We made it from my place to Consolidated's parking lot in about three minutes, Barnes merely slowing down for red lights.

Then came the big giggle of the night, or rather morning. Tomlinson wouldn't let us in.

"I'm sorry, sir. I know you, Mr. Barnes, but I have strict orders. No one is to be admitted to the premises after closing time unless accompanied by a company executive."

Barnes did some stewing and fretting and talking to the cop who was on duty, a young guy named Freiberg whose cheeks were beginning to show some five o'clock shadow. Freiberg said Shunk would have to arrange it. As sleepy as I was, the idea of calling Shunk at 4 A.M. gave me a laugh.

We walked up to the all-night Automat across from Grand Central, Barnes muttering all the way, and had breakfast. That took about half an hour. I went out and bought two copies of the *Times*. We read newspapers and had three more cups of coffee. Barnes had decided he would wait until six o'clock to call Shunk, as Shunk probably got up about that time anyway.

Barnes lowered his newspaper. "Sometimes I think I have streaks of genuine clairvoyance. This morning, out of the blue, I had this startling vision of the inside of the Coke machine with the cans removed and the channels stuffed with money."

"Yeah," I said, going back to Tom Wicker. Then: "I still don't see why he would move the money to the Coke machine."

"I'll explain it to you. It would be such a beautifully simple way of getting the entire haul out of the building quickly." He scribbled in his cigarette notebook and then lit one. "A couple of guys show up with a truck and a dolly and say they're from the vending company and are there to take away the broken machine for repair. The police have already checked it, so out it goes."

"Yeah." I should have thought of that. Maybe losing all that blood was making me stupid. But suppose the people from the *real* vending machine company showed up before it was arranged? Still, if Tip, Gates, or Ryan were involved, they could probably control that.

Barnes telephoned Shunk at six. He was a bit annoyed, because he generally didn't get up until seven. He agreed to meet us at Consolidated as soon as he could make it, which would probably be about eight.

We went back to Barnes's Porsche and sat in it. I dozed while he nervously drummed his fingers on the steering wheel and smoked. At seven he got out of the car and went to call Dale Jones.

By ten of eight, both Jones and Shunk had

arrived. We went up to the second floor of the still deserted building and looked at the Coke machine. If it turned out to be empty, Barnes would probably have a nervous breakdown. Preventive medicine was required. I gave him two tranquilizers and said, "Now eat those, don't put them in your pocket."

Shunk fiddled with the lock for a moment or two and opened it easily. We all crowded close to look. It was absolutely loaded with green stuff.

Jones was ecstatic. "I've got to eat humble pie, old boy," he said to Barnes. "I was about to cancel you out."

Barnes smiled.

"I like a man who sticks to his guns when he's sure he's right," said Shunk.

Barnes continued to smile, as though in a happy dream. Then he snapped out of it. "One thing I'd like to point out. This isn't going to help us much in proving who put it there. My suggestion is that we leave it in the machine, and watch where it goes."

Jones removed his ever present pipe. "Oh no, you don't, my lad. That money is going to be inventoried and then put in a vault."

Shunk shook his head. "Barnes is right."

Jones stuck out his lower lip. "Sorry, old boy. My company is on the hook for one half million dollars. I am not willing to risk it."

Shunk snapped his fingers. "We've got a

truckload of counterfeit stuff." He headed for a telephone, saying, "If we can make the switch before anyone gets here, we're in business."

In about fifteen minutes we heard a siren squealing as a squad car pulled into the consolidated lot. Gaines came puffing up the steps with a suitcase. We quickly unloaded the real stuff and filled the machine with counterfeit bills. Jones and Gaines packed the robbery haul into the now empty suitcase, and left to head for the district attorney's office. Barnes had been right about getting at the situation early. Since Tomlinson had remained at the door with Freiberg, no one connected with Consolidated had witnessed the discovery. But we only missed by minutes. Less than five minutes after Jones left with the money, Consolidated employees began to arrive.

"Hurry up and wait," I said. "Now we wait and wait."

"I don't think we'll wait long," said Barnes. "He must be desperate to get the stuff out of here."

Shunk busied himself arranging to cover the departure of the Coke machine from all angles.

I stationed myself in the small lobby on the first floor. I drank more coffee and waited, chatting with the receptionist and staring through the glass doors at the street.

Slightly before ten a panel truck double-parked in front of the building. Two men in white coveralls climbed out. One of them was my friend Marcel Proust from the Gay-Itty Theatre. I hurried up the stairs. If he caught sight of me, it would queer the whole deal. And I wasn't punning.

I rushed into Barnes's office. "They're here to pick up the machine. A couple of Tip Horgan's friends from the theater in the Village.'

He beamed, reaching for his cigarettes. "Sheer clairvoyance. I must learn to cultivate it."

"Sheer shrewd thinking," I said, getting tangled up on the second word. "You don't need clairvoyance."

We walked to the front of the building and watched from the window while the two men dollied the Coke machine out to the truck. They had prepared for their roles well. The white coveralls had red lettering spelling out, "Dombrowsky Vending, Inc."

Barnes could have been a New York cab driver. In the Porsche we made it the Gay-Itty before the truck and its escort of squad cars got there. Barnes found a parking place a half block away on the other side of the street. We could see the entrance.

The truck arrived, double-parked, and the Coke machine was dollied into the theater.

Shunk poked his head into the window. "I'm giving them ten minutes to open it and gloat, then we bust in and catch them red-handed. The place is completely surrounded."

I glanced automatically at my watch.

The rickety old door was locked, but it only took one of the heavy-set cops a second to snap it open with a heave of his shoulder. Shunk, seven cops with revolvers drawn, Barnes, and I crowded into the small lobby. The Coke machine was there, ready to serve patrons of the Gay-Itty. Horgan, Marcel Proust, and the third member of the team were sitting on the floor counting the counterfeit bills. The hundreds in one stack, the fifties in another, and so on.

Horgan saw us first. He dropped his stack of money, jumped up, and ran into the theater. Three of the cops went after him. The other grabbed Marcel Proust and his friend.

The sound of firing reverberated deafeningly through the old building. Barnes, Shunk, and I hurried into the theater.

One cop was crouched behind a seat, firing in the direction of the stage. Somewhere up there in the dark, Horgan was returning his fire. We quickly dropped behind seats.

"Give yourself up, Horgan. You haven't got a chance," yelled Shunk.

Horgan's answer was another ear-splitting bang.

"The place is surrounded, Horgan. Give it up," called Shunk.

Another voice up near the stage yelled, "Cease fire!"

"Whatta you mean, Cease fire!" yelled Shunk.

"He's immobilized, Lieutenant."

Someone found some lights, and the small auditorium was suddenly brightly illuminated in its pathetic seediness. We made our way cautiously to the front.

Horgan was lying just off the stage, a good half of his head blown away.

Shunk said to the cop who had called "Cease fire," "Good shot in the dark."

"I didn't get him, Lieutenant. I think he turned the gun on himself. The flash was right where he is."

There was nothing anyone could do for Horgan. We went back to the lobby to wait for the medical examiner.

Marcel Proust was sitting on the floor, handcuffed, tears streaming down his cheeks. "He's dead. I know he's dead." He rocked slowly back and forth in an agony of grief.

"He killed himself," said Shunk. "We didn't—"

"He *said* he would if he didn't pull it off."

Shunk squatted down beside him. "He was your friend—your lover, wasn't he?"

Marcel bowed his head, wiping his cheeks awkwardly with the backs of his handcuffed hands. "If people would just leave us *alone*," he said, his voice trembling.

"Why in God's name did he do such a crazy, stupid thing?" Shunk asked.

Marcel continued to stare at the floor, bleary-eyed. "I begged him. I pleaded with him not to."

"With his future—he had the whole world in his pocket," said Shunk. "He would have been the head of a billion-dollar corporation—"

"He had no future. Sooner or later the old man would have found out. It was a straitjacket. He couldn't stand living that way. He would have been in a real one before long," said Marcel. He sniffed loudly then fumbled awkwardly with the pocket of his jeans and managed with two hands to pull out a handkerchief. He wiped his eyes and blew his nose. "Tip thought he was entitled to that money. His share of the estate would be a hundred times bigger. Old Ellsworth didn't earn it, you know. *His* grandfather did. There were no income taxes in those days. The old man had no *right* to cut Tip off."

Shunk helped him to his feet. "It wasn't very decent of him to frame Bob Cressett."

Marcel swayed dizzily. Shunk caught his arm quickly and steadied him. "It was just a red herring to confuse the issue. Tip figured they'd never convict him."

"Some red herring. We'd certainly have a tough time convicting him, all right. Why in hell did he kill him?"

Marcel, who had been holding his handkerchief wadded in one hand, blew his nose again. "He didn't mean to kill anybody, Wicher *or* Cressett. He was wearing a ski mask, and Wicher couldn't have identified him. He could have shot Wicher when Wicher reached for his gun. In-

290

stead he tapped him on the head, just to knock him out. He was terribly depressed when he found out Wicher had died."

Barnes, who had been listening to the exchange, said, "But why Cressett?"

"He was trying to blackmail Tip. He knew nothing about Tip's involvement into the robbery, but he did know Tip was gay, and he knew Tip was General Ellsworth's grandson. He sent word that if Tip didn't help him get off the hook, he would tell the General." He paused and looked around wearily. "Will one of you fellows give me a butt, please?"

Barnes handed him a cigarette and lit it for him.

"You can see the position Tip was in. What was he supposed to do, go to his grandfather and say, 'Make the police lay off my friend Cressett, who seems to be involved in the robbery'? Tip went over to have it out with him." He puffed on the cigarette for a few seconds, inhaling deeply. "He didn't mean to kill him, just teach him a lesson. Nothing makes us as homicidally angry as blackmail."

"You helped him with the robbery, I suppose," said Shunk in a soft voice.

It was the wrong tack. Marcel eyed Shunk coldly. The question had penetrated his emotional befuddlement and set alarm signals working. "I'm not talking any more until I have a lawyer," he said.

Barnes and I adjourned to Luchow's for lunch.

Over Plymouth Gin martinis, Barnes said, "The lot of the homosexual is not an easy one." He sighed deeply. "I suppose the pressures can become unbearable."

I ordered a second martini. I mean, Barnes was giving me the afternoon off, no less. "I wonder if Tip handled the robbery all alone."

He could have. When Shunk gets through with Marcel Proust and his friends, we may know."

"I want you to find a home for that mutt. She's puddling all over my apartment. I don't know anything about housebreaking dogs."

Barnes was apologetic. He gave me detailed instructions on how to housebreak dogs.